THE COMMON LAW LIBRARY

THE LIBRARY

University of Ulster at Magee

Due Back (subject to recall)

Fines will apply to items returned after due date

THE COMMON LAW LIBRARY

PHIPSON ON EVIDENCE

FIRST SUPPLEMENT
TO THE
SEVENTEENTH EDITION

Up to date until
September 2011

SWEET & MAXWELL

 THOMSON REUTERS

First Edition	(1892)	By Sidney L. Phipson
Second Edition	(1898)	" "
Third Edition	(1902)	" "
Fourth Edition	(1907)	" "
Fifth Edition	(1911)	" "
Sixth Edition	(1921)	" "
Seventh Edition	(1930)	By Roland Burrows
Eighth Edition	(1942)	By Roland Burrows, K.C.
Ninth Edition	(1952)	By Sir Roland Burrows
Second Impression	(1959)	" "
Tenth Edition	(1963)	By Michael V. Argyle, Q.C.
Eleventh Edition	(1970)	By John Buzzard
		Roy Amlot
		Stephen Mitchell
Twelfth Edition	(1976)	By John Buzzard
		Richard May
		M. N. Howard
Thirteenth Edition	(1982)	By John Buzzard
		Richard May
		M. N. Howard
Fourteenth Edition	(1990)	By M. N. Howard, Q.C.
		Peter Crane
		Daniel Hochberg
Fifteenth Edition	(2000)	By M. N. Howard, Q.C.
		and Specialist Editors
First Supplement	(2002)	By M. N. Howard, Q.C.
		and Specialist Editors
Second Supplement	(2002)	By Hodge M. Malek, Q.C.
		and Specialist Editors
Third Supplement	(2003)	By Hodge M. Malek, Q.C.
		and Specialist Editors
Sixteenth Edition	(2005)	By Hodge M. Malek, Q.C.
		and Specialist Editors
First Supplement	(2007)	By Hodge M. Malek, Q.C.
		and Specialist Editors
Second Supplement	(2008)	By Hodge M. Malek, Q.C.
		and Specialist Editors
Seventeenth Edition	(2010)	By Hodge M. Malek, Q.C.
		and Specialist Editors
First Supplement	(2011)	By Hodge M. Malek, Q.C.
		and Specialist Editors

Published in 2011 by Sweet & Maxwell, 100 Avenue Road, London NW3 3PF
part of Thomson Reuters (Professional) UK Limited
(Registered in England & Wales, Company No 1679046.
Registered Office and address for service:
Aldgate House, 33 Aldgate High Street, London EC3N 1DL)
Typeset by Servis Filmsetting Ltd, Offerton, Stockport
Printed and bound in Great Britain by Ashford Colour Press Ltd, Gosport, Hants
For further information on our products and services, visit:
www.sweetandmaxwell.co.uk

ISBN 978-0-41404-777-8

No natural forests were destroyed to make this product;
only farmed timber was used and replanted.

A CIP catalogue record for this book is available from the British Library.

HOW TO USE THIS SUPPLEMENT

This is the First Supplement to the Seventeenth Edition of
Phipson on Evidence, and has been compiled according to the
structure of the main volume.

At the beginning of each chapter of this Supplement is a mini table
of contents from the main volume. Where a heading in this table of
contents has been marked with a square pointer, this indicates that there is
relevant information in the Supplement to which the reader should refer.
Material that is new to the Cumulative Supplement is indicated by the
symbol ■.

Within each chapter, updating information is referenced to
the relevant paragraph in the main volume.

PREFACE

The length of the first supplement to the seventeenth edition is testimony to the continuing developments in the law of evidence. For example, there have been a number of significant cases on the use of hearsay evidence under the Criminal Justice Act 2003. This supplement identifies and comments upon such developments, which will be of real assistance to practitioners and academics alike.

The effect and importance of the Human Rights Act 1998 in the sphere of evidence has continued apace, with decisions specifically in the areas of public hearings, anonymous witnesses, the use of hearsay evidence and legal professional privilege. The use of bad character as part of the Prosecution case law is another area in which there has been much recent development, hence the extensive and detailed account in Chapter 19. These are just some of the many developments.

I am grateful to all of the specialist editors for their hard work in producing this supplement. Every chapter has been reviewed by at least one other member of the team apart from the allocated editor, and also reviewed by myself. I would also like to thank all those at Sweet & Maxwell who have helped to produce this supplement, especially Gregory Smith, Sophie Lawler and Stephanie Hulme.

The law stated in this supplement is up to date until September 30, 2011; however some authorities from October 2011 have been added at the proof stage.

HODGE M. MALEK Q.C.
Gray's Inn
October 31, 2011

TABLE OF CASES

TABLE OF STATUTES

TABLE OF STATUTORY INSTRUMENTS

TABLE OF CIVIL PROCEDURE RULES

TABLE OF EUROPEAN AND INTERNATIONAL CONVENTIONS AND LEGISLATION

TABLE OF PRACTICE DIRECTIONS

PACE CODE OF PRACTICE D

CHAPTER 1

INTRODUCTION

5.—FUNCTIONS OF JUDGE AND JURY

A judge has a power to discharge a jury on the grounds of jury tampering and **1–27** to continue the trial on his own under s.46 of the Criminal Justice Act 2003: *R v. Guthrie* [2011] EWCA Crim 1338, [2011] 2 Cr. App. R.20 (judge discharged jury and continued trial on her own). However great care should be taken in deciding whether the judge himself should continue alone in an on-going trial, particularly where he has seen evidence not put before the jury (such as public interest immunity material prejudicial to the defendant): *R v. S(K)* [2010] 1 Cr. App. R.20 (conviction by judge set aside on ground of legitimate perception of apparent judicial bias).

The right to trial by jury is not a right protected by the European Convention of Human Rights and can be circumscribed by statute. In a case of jury tampering a judge may order a trial by judge alone and there is no requirement to disclose all the material to the defence relating to alleged jury tampering: *R v. Twomey (No.2)* [2011] EWCA Crim 8, [2011] 1 Cr. App. R.29.

7.—IMPACT OF THE HUMAN RIGHTS ACT

(c) *Specific areas of evidence law*

(iii) *Articles 6: fair trial rights generally*

fn.292 See *HM Advocate v Murtagh (John)* [2009] UKPC 36, [2011] 1 AC 731 PC (SC) **1–62** where the Court held that a defendant's right to fair trial under Art.6 ECHR required only the disclosure of such previous convictions of Crown witnesses as may materially weaken the Crown's case or strengthen that of the defence.

(iv) *Public hearings (articles 2, 5, 6, 8 and 10)*

1–74   The principles of open justice do not extend to a right to public or press to inspect documents or other exhibits placed before a court in criminal proceedings: *R. (Guardian News and Media Ltd) v. City of Westminster Magistrates' Court and USA* [2010] EWHC 3376 (Admin), [2011] 1 Cr. App. R.36.

(v) *Anonymous Witnesses*

1–75   The court's power to make a witness anonymity order is now conferred by the Coroners and Justice Act 2009. For the procedure, see Part 29 of the Criminal Procedure Rules 2011 and Consolidated Criminal Practice Direction (Amendment No.24) (Criminal Proceedings: Witness Anonymity Order (2); Forms) [2010] 2 Cr. App. R. 6.

(vi) *Examination and adducing of witnesses (article 6(3)(d))*

1–77   In *R v. Horncastle and Blackmore* [2009] UKSC 14, [2010] 1 Cr. App. R. 17, the Supreme Court declined to apply the sole or decisive evidence test adopted by the European Court of Human Rights in *Al Khawaji and Tahery v. United Kingdom* (2009) 49 E.H.R.R. 1. The statutory regime under s.116 of the Criminal Justice Act 2003 for the admission of statements of unavailable witnesses enacted exceptions to the hearsay rule which contain safeguards to protect a defendant against unfair prejudice. That statutory regime was found to render unnecessary the sole or decisive rule. Thus, provided the 2003 Act was observed, there would be no breach of art.6(3)(d) merely because a conviction was based solely or to a decisive extent on hearsay evidence. See also M. Requa, 'Absent Witnesses and the UK Supreme Court: judicial deference as judicial dialogue?' (2010) 14 E&P 208–231; I. Jones, 'A political judgment? Reconciling hearsay and the right to challenge' (2010) 14 E&P 232–252.

(vii) *New evidence on appeal (article 6)*

1–78   The rule against any investigation or inquiry into jury deliberations is subject to two narrow exceptions. First, if it emerges that there may have been a complete repudiation of the oath taken by the jury to try the case according to the evidence. Second, where extraneous material has been introduced into the jury deliberations. Guidance must be given to the jury to ensure so far as practicable that they do not see or take account of extraneous material, such as on the internet: *R v. Thompson* [2010] EWCA Crim 1623, [2010] 2 Cr. App. R. 27; *R v. McDonnell* [2010] EWCA Crim 2352, [2011] 1 Cr. App. R. 28.

(ix) *Legal professional privilege (articles 6 and 8)*

1–81   fn.180 The requirement that a defendant file a defence case statement within the meaning of s.6A of the Criminal Procedure and Investigations Act 1996, does not mean that the defendant is obliged to disclose his confidential discussions with his advocate, nor is he required to incriminate himself: *R v. Rochford* [2010] EWCA Crim. 1928, [2011] 1 Cr. App. R.11 at [21].

(xi) *Hearsay*

fn.396 The Supreme Court declined to follow *Al Khawaji and Tahery v. United*   **1–83**
Kingdom (2009) 49 E.H.R.R. 1 in *R v. Horncastle and Blackmore* [2009] UKSC 14,
[2010] 1 Cr. App. R.17 (see under para.1–77 above).

In *Abrose v Harris* [2011] UKSC 43, the Supreme Court held that in respect of two
of the appellants (Ambrose and M) the use of questions in response to police questions, given by the roadside (A) and the use of an admission made at his home in the
presence of the police (M), without the benefit of legal access prior to the giving of the
evidence, was not incompatible with art.6(1).

In respect of G, because he was detained and handcuffed, the circumstances were
sufficiently coercive for the incriminating answers he gave to questions put without
access to legal advice, for these answers to be inadmissible.

Finally, in *HM Advocate v P* [2011] UKSC 44, the court held that the use of evidence obtained from information disclosed during a police interview without having
access to legal advice was not incompatible with art.6(1). Whether the use of evidence
obtained from P's friend, who was interviewed as a result of P's response in interview
was incompatible with art.6(1), was a matter for the trial judge.

THE DEFINING OF THE ISSUES

2.—STATEMENTS OF CASE AND PLEADINGS

(a) *Civil Cases*

The importance of pleadings was stressed in *Canberra Data v. Vibe Constructions*   **2–02**
[2010] ACTSC 20, (2010) 173 ACTR 33. Where an issue has not been raised in the
pleadings, the court may refuse to allow a new point to be raised late in the trial:
Lombard North Central Plc v. Automobile World (UK) Ltd [2010] EWCA Civ 20,
CA.
   fn.7 Where there is more than one defendant, it is permissible to serve differently
worded particulars of claim on each defendant: *Tetra Pak Ltd v. Biddle & Co* [2010]
EWHC 54 (Ch), [2010] 1 W.L.R. 1466, Ch.D.

(b) *Criminal Cases*

The form, content, signature and service of indictments is now covered in the   **2–03**
Criminal Procedure Rules 2011, Pt.14, and Practice Direction (Criminal Proceedings:
Arraignment) [2008] 1 W.L.R. 154. It is important to remove from the indictment for
trial unnecessary counts. Those added as a makeweight should be stripped out. In *R.
v. N(P)* [2010] EWCA Crim 941, [2010] 2 Cr. App. R. 14 at [19], having stressed the
level of care with which indictments should be drafted, the Court of Appeal went on
to state:

> "No less important, when it becomes clear that a case is to proceed as a trial,
> counsel for the prosecution and the judge should reflect on which count or counts
> should be presented to the jury. This requires close attention to the realities of the
> case and none at all to the theoretical legal possibilities which may arise. It also
> requires careful attention to the criminality which has resulted in the case coming
> to trial, as well as the evidence to support the allegation. Finally, it requires the
> avoidance of duplication and the risk of unnecessary complications both for the
> jury and for the judge, and the ultimate wasting of scarce and valuable resources.
> Unnecessary counts should be stripped out of the indictment. If that does not take
> place at the plea and case management hearing, or any of the earlier interlocutory
> proceedings, it must take place when the trial is due to begin and before the jury
> is sworn."

fn.26 Whilst an indictment should be signed and dated (Crim PR r.14.1(3)), this is no longer a statutory requirement, hence their absence does not invalidate the indictment. Coroners and Justice Act 2009 s.116.(1) abolished the rule that a bill of indictment only became an indictment upon its being signed.

3.—VARIANCE AND AMENDMENT

(a) *Civil Cases*

2–06   fn.41 Add *Swain-Mason v. Mills & Reeve* [2011] EWCA Civ 14 (late amendment at trial refused).

fn.42 Add *Groveholt Ltd v. Hughes* [2010] EWCA Civ 538; *Carey Group plc v. AIB Group (UK) Plc* [2011] EWHC 594 (Ch).

fn.44 CPR, r.17.4(2). Add *Berezovsky v. Abramovich* [2011] EWCA Civ 153 (claim amended to seek restitution of assets).

2–07   fn.56 In relation to CPR r.19.5(3) (adding or substituting a party after the end of the relevant limitation period) where it is said that the new party to be substituted for the party was named in the claim in mistake for the new party, it is not necessary for the court to be satisfied that the mistake was not misleading to the other party or did not cause reasonable doubt as to the party intended to be sued. It is possible that these factors may be relevant to discretion: *Lockheed Martin Corporation v. Willis Group Ltd* [2010] EWCA Civ 927, CA.

fn.58 In relation to CPR r.19.5(3)(b) (adding or substituting a party after the end of the relevant limitation period) where it is said that the claim cannot be properly carried on unless the new party is added or substituted, the relevant claim is the existing claim: c.f. *Roberts & Gill & Co* [2010] UKSC 22, [2010] 2 W.L.R. 1227, SC, where proceedings were commenced in a personal capacity and permission was refused to continue the proceedings in a representative capacity under a derivative claim on behalf of the estate.

(b) *Criminal Cases*

2–09   In *R v. Leeks* [2009] EWCA Crim 1612, [2010] 1 Cr. App. R.5 at trial it had been assumed that the indictment had been amended, when in fact no order had been made under the Indictments Act 1915, s.5. The conviction was set aside on appeal as the failure to comply with s.5(1) meant that the charge had never been validly added to the indictment.

fn.68 Add *R v. Brooker* [2011] EWCA Crim 7, [2011] 1 Cr. App. R.26, CA (co-conspirator added to indictment for purpose of retrial of a defendant whose original conviction set aside on appeal).

JUDICIAL NOTICE

2—SCOPE OF THE GENERAL RULE

Outside the context of particular specialist tribunals, a judge should not use his own experience to decide that there has been a specific breach of duty and its causative effect in the particular case: *Dasreef v. Hawchar* [2011] HCA 21, (2011) 277 A.L.R. 611 at [142], HC (Aus). **3–05**

8—NOTORIOUS FACTS

fn.184 In *R. v. Ahmed and Ahmed* [2011] EWCA Crim 184 at [58] the Court of Appeal commented that a time may come when judicial notice may be taken of generally accepted facts about Al Qaeda, but that time had not yet been reached. **3–17**

ADMISSIONS

4.—INFORMAL ADMISSIONS—CLIENT, SOLICITOR, COUNSEL AND WITNESSES

(b) *Criminal cases*

In *R (Firth) v Epping Magistrates' Court* [2011] EWHC 388 (Admin) the accused **4–24** was charged with assault occasioning actual bodily harm. Counsel (on her behalf) had completed a case progression form in accordance with the Criminal Procedure Rules 2010, stating that the accused had acted in self-defence. At the committal proceedings, the defence attempted to argue that the prosecution witness statements did not establish a prima facie case because they did not identify the accused as the person who had allegedly committed the assault. The magistrates relied upon the statement in the progression form as evidence of the accused's involvement. It was contended that such a case management document was not covered by the common law principles in relation to admissions made by agents expounded in *R v Turner* [1975] 61 Cr. App. R. 67, and that to admit it would infringe the principle against self-incrimination. However, Toulson LJ ruled that there was nothing inherently repugnant in requiring the nature of the defence to be made plain well before trial, and if there was any unfairness in admitting it at the trial, the accused's position would be protected by the exclusionary discretionary under s.78 of the Police and Criminal Evidence Act 1984. The admissibility of the case progression form at a pre-trial hearing was consistent with the object of the Criminal Procedure Rules s.69(4), namely further the interests of justice, do fairness and encourage expedition. Earlier cases in the field such as *R v. Hutchinson* (1986) 82 Cr. App. R. 51 and *Diedrich and Aldridge* [1997] 1 Cr. App. R. 361 were decided when the system of the administration of criminal justice was very different.

ESTOPPELS

1.—INTRODUCTORY

(c) *Restrictions on estoppels*

fn.21 The most recent edition of *Cross and Tapper on Evidence* is the 11th edn **5–03** (2007).

fn.39 For an analysis of the wider approach of the Australian courts to the law of estoppel, particularly promissory and equitable estoppel, see *Waltons Stores (Interstate) Ltd v Maher* [1988] HCA 7; (1988) 164 CLR 387; see also *Tipperary Developments Pty Ltd v The State Of Western Australia* [2009] WASCA 126 which considers the relationship of estoppel and s.4 of the Statute of Frauds 1677.

(d) *Classifications and possible underlying principles*

fn.82 See also *Tipperary Developments Pty Ltd v The State of Western Australia* **5–06** [2009] WASCA 126.

2.—LEGAL ESTOPPELS

(b) *Estoppels by record and by res judicata*

fn.99 S.268 of the Copyright, Design and Patents Act 1988 is now repealed: Sch.2 **5–08** of The Registered Designs Regulations 2001 No. 3949.

(c) *Estoppels by deed*

fn.111 See *Iesini & Ors v Westrip Holdings Ltd & Ors* [2009] EWHC 2526 (Ch); **5–09** [2010] BCC 420 at [97] for an example of the limits of estoppel by convention in the context of a failure to obtain a special resolution of the company as required by the Companies Act 1985.

(d) *Estoppels in pais (or by conduct)*

(i) *From agreement*

5–21   fn.163 See now *Byles on Bills of Exchange and Cheques* 27th edn (2007) paras 17–006—17–010.

fn.164 See now *Byles on Bills of Exchange and Cheques* 27th edn (2007) para.20–027.

fn.165 See now *Byles on Bills of Exchange and Cheques* 27th edn (2007) paras 32–008—32–014.

(iv) *From silence, omission or acquiescence*

5–31   fn.251 In *Greenwood v. Martins Bank Ltd* [1933] A.C. 51 the plaintiff sued for repayment of monies paid out of his account by the defendant bank on cheques forged by his wife. The plaintiff owed a duty to the bank to disclose his wife's forgeries of his cheques and having failed to do so he was estopped from asserting that the signatures to the cheques were forgeries. The husband's silence in the face of the admitted duty to disclose the forgery amounted to a representation.

A similar result would have been arrived at in *English v English & Anor* [2010] EWHC 2058 (Ch) a case actually decided in ratification. The claimant was estopped from denying the execution of a legal charge which her son had forged. To protect her son from the risk of prosecution the claimant failed to notify the mortgagee of the fact of the forgery when she became aware of it, had discussions with the mortgagee about arrears and failed to raise any objection to the validity of the charge when she later made arrangements for redemption. The failure of the claimant to notify the claimant before redemption meant that the mortgagee had lost the right to apply for an indemnity to H.M. Land Registry.

A banker's silence may also give rise to an estoppel. In *ING Bank NV v Ros Roca SA* [2011] EWCA Civ 353 the claimant bank agreed to provide certain advice to the defendant in the proposed acquisition of a another company. The fee for that advice depended upon the value of the company. The bank's engagement letter made specific reference to a valuation formula with a date of 2006 but the transaction did not take place until the end of 2007. There was however a shared assumption that the 2006 formula would not be used so that an estoppel by convention or acquiescence was established. The bank knew that the assumed amount of transaction costs was irredeemably inconsistent with a calculation of the fees based on the 2006 formula.

It was held that it would be unjust or unconscionable to allow the bank to go back on that assumption. It did not depend on the precise terms of the agreement, nor whether they gave rise to, or negated, a "duty to speak" on the part of bank. It was enough that the bank and the client were engaged in a joint project, in which each was entitled to assume that the other would act consistently, and would not knowingly conceal information of significance to the project or their relationship in it. The client was entitled to expect its financial adviser to act "honestly and responsibly" to have taken steps to make its position known. By contrast with the facts in *Republic of India v. India Steamship Co (No 2) (The "Indian Endurance")* [1998] AC 878, these were "special circumstances" which required the bank to do more than simply acquiesce in its client's continued use of a calculation which they believed, or had reason to believe, was wrong: see the judgment of Carnwath LJ [71].

(vi) *From waiver*

fn.266 Chitty on Contracts, 30th edn (2008) 24–007.   **5–33**

3.—EQUITABLE ESTOPPELS

(b) *Equitable proprietary estoppel*

While Lord Walker in *Stack v. Dowden* [2007] 2 AC 432 at [37] drew attention to **5–37** the need to keep the distinction between proprietary estoppel and constructive trust, Arden LJ noted at [56] in *Herbert v Doyle & Anor* [2010] EWCA Civ 1095 that it appeared from *Cobbe v Yeoman's Row Management Ltd* [2008] 1 WLR 1752 that, in some situations at least, both doctrines have a requirement for completeness of agreement with respect to an interest in property. In *Herbert v Doyle & Anor* the claimant succeeded in obtaining an order requiring the defendants to convey three freehold parking spaces pursuant to an oral agreement which created a constructive trust.

fn.292 *Thorner v Major and ors* [2009] UKHL 18; [2009] 1 W.L.R. 776   **5–38**
fn.293 *Thorner v Major and ors* [2009] UKHL 18; [2009] 1 W.L.R. 776

fn.296 *Bye v Colvin-Scott* [2010] W.T.L.R. 1   **5–39**

fn.316 *Bye v Colvin-Scott* [2010] W.T.L.R. 1   **5–41**
fn.317 On appeal: *Hopper v Hopper* [2008] EWCA Civ 1417, appeal allowed to a limited extent, but not on this point.

(c) *Promissory estoppel*

fn.335 *Chitty on Contracts* 30th edn (2008), 3–085—3–107.   **5–44**

fn.357 See also *Tipperary Developments Pty Ltd v The State Of Western Australia* **5–47** [2009] WASCA 126 per McLure J.A. at [132]—[145].

BURDEN AND STANDARD OF PROOF

2.—BURDEN OF PROOF IN CIVIL CASES

(c) *Examples*

Lombard North Central Plc v Automobile World (UK) Ltd [2010] EWCA Civ 20 **6–08(d)** (CA Civ Div) confirming 6–08(d), the Court of Appeal held that since the party in breach ordinarily places the other party in a difficult situation, the burden of proof is on the party in breach to demonstrate a failure on the part of the other party to mitigate loss (para.72).

3.—BURDEN OF PROOF IN CRIMINAL CASES

(d) *Satisfying the evidential burden*

Mr Farid Yeganeh v Zurich Plc, Zurich Insurance Company [2010] EWHC 1185 **6–14** (QB) (High Court of Justice, QBD London Mercantile Court): applying *Rhesa Shipping Co SA v Edmunds (The Popi M)* [1985] 1 WLR 948 (HL), Judge Mackie QC found that Zurich had not proved that Mr Yeganeh committed an act of arson. In the absence of "sound evidence of a motive" (para.55) to burn down the said house, and direct evidence of arson, Zurich had not discharged the criminal burden of proof.

4.—PRESUMPTIONS

(d) *Examples of presumptions of law*

(ix) *Due preformance of public or official acts*

Doli incapax

6–29   R v H [2010] EWCA Crim 312: concept of doli incapax still applies to offences alleged to have been committed prior to the coming into force of s.34 of the Crime and Disorder Act 1998.

(e) *Res ipsa loquitur*

6–30   *George v Eagle Air Services Ltd* [2009] UKPC 21, [2009] 1 WLR 2133 (PC (StL)) doctrine of res ipsa loquitur applicable to air crashes. The Privy Council (St Lucia) reasoned that such crashes did not ordinarily occur in the absence of default by someone connected to the aircraft's design, manufacture or operation (paras 12–14, 17). Therefore, the defendants had "failed to displace the inference of negligence which results from the crash itself" (para.13).

5.—IMPACT OF THE HUMAN RIGHTS ACT ON REVERSE BURDENS AND PRESUMPTIONS

(b) *Specific categories of cases*

(ii) *Reverse burdens as to states of knowledge: less serious criminal and regulatory offences*

6–42   *Regina v Webster* [2010] EWCA Crim 2819, [2011] 1 Cr App R 16 (Court of Appeal, Crim Div): the reverse burden of proof per s.2 of the Prevention of Corruption Act 1916, which places the burden on public servant defendants to prove that any gifts received by them were not given corruptly, was held to unjustifiably interfere with the presumption of innocence in Art.6 ECHR. As such, the Court of Appeal read down s.2, placing the legal burden on the Crown to prove to the criminal standard that the gift was corruptly made (paras 23–32).

(iv) *Regulatory offences and reasonable steps*

6–46   Applying *R v Chargot Ltd (t/a Contract Services)* [2008] UKHL 73, the Court of Appeal (Criminal Division) in R v Hutchins (Anthony) [2011] EWCA Crim 1056 held that the defendants had committed an offence under s.23 of the Private Security Industry Act 2001 in knowing that guards employed by them were unlicensed—the prosecution did not have to prove specific knowledge of each individual offence.

6.—STANDARD OF PROOF: CRIMINAL CASES

(b) *Meaning of "beyond reasonable doubt"*

In *R (Adams) v Secretary of State for Justice* [2011] UKSC 18, [2011] 2 WLR 1180,   **6–51**
the Supreme Court ruled that entitlement to compensation per s.133 Criminal Justice
Act 1988 was not restricted to those who had established beyond reasonable doubt
that they were innocent of the crime for which they were convicted. It was sufficient
to show a new fact which so undermined the evidence against the defendant that no
conviction could possibly have been based upon it.

In *McDonald & Ors v HM Advocate* [2010] HCJAC 95 the High Court of Justiciary
held that even where evidence of a Crown witness was not relied upon due to its
lack of credibility, the jury remained entitled to return a guilty verdict against two
men convicted of murder since all the evidence, when viewed together, produced a
coherent picture allowing for the conclusion of guilt beyond reasonable doubt.

In *R v Majid (Abdul)* [2009] EWCA Crim 2563 the favoured phrase used to direct
juries, that they must be sure the accused is guilty, is designed to avoid difficulties
juries encounter with the concept of beyond reasonable doubt. Whilst the trial judge
ought to have used the Judicial Studies Board specimen direction regarding the standard of proof when directing the jury, instead of directing them that the standard was
satisfaction of guilty beyond all reasonable doubt, it could not be said that the jury
had been so confused so as to apply the wrong standard.

Applying *R v Makuwa* [2006] EWCA Crim 175, the court in *R v AM* [2010] EWCA
Crim 2400, [2011] 1 Cr App 35 held that anyone charged with the offence of having
in their possession a false identity document upon entering the United Kingdom,
contrary to s.25(1) of the Identity Cards Act 2006, is entitled "to adduce sufficient
material to raise an issue that he or she is a refugee" and thereby entitled to protection
under s.31 of the Immigration and Asylum Act 1999.

Steel v The State of Western Australia [2010] WASCA 118 (30 June 2010) confirming that the prosecution bears the legal burden of proving that the accused did not act
in self-defence, the Supreme Court of Western Australia held that the trial judge had
not misled or confused the jury as to the burden of proof.

7.—STANDARD OF PROOF: CIVIL CASES

(b) *Serious or criminal allegations and quasi-criminal proceedings*

In *Re C and D (children)* [2010] EWHC 3714 applying the rule in *Re B (Children)*   **6–56**
[2008] UKHL 35, the burden of proof in such cases rests upon the local authority and
the standard of proof is the balance of probability (para.179). On the facts, the local
authority failed to establish that the harm done to the children was non-accidental.

Chapter 7

RELEVANCE, ADMISSIBILITY AND WEIGHT: PREVIOUS AND SUBSEQUENT EXISTENCE OF FACTS: THE BEST EVIDENCE RULE

4.—Relevance and Admissibility

(b) *Sufficient relevance*

In *HSBC Asia Holdings BV v Gillespie* [2011] I.C.R. 192 EAT, Underhill J **7–07** (President) held that employment tribunals have power to exclude evidence which is "'logically' or 'theoretically' relevant but nevertheless too marginal, or otherwise unlikely to assist the court, for its admission to be justified" (at [13]). He cited the relevant passage in *Phipson on Evidence*, 17th edn (2010) §7–07 but rejected the opinion expressed there to the effect that it is better to ask whether the evidence has sufficient weight or sufficient probative value rather than whether it has sufficient relevance.

(e) *Multiple relevance*

One of the examples given in the text of evidence that is admissible for one purpose **7–12** but not another is no longer a clear example: in *certain circumstances* an out-of-court confession by an accused may now be admissible evidence against a co-accused who is implicated by it; for example, when it has been admitted against him for that purpose under Criminal Justice Act 2003, s.114(1)(d).

(f) *Illustrations of relevance*

(i) *Relevance of possession of cash in drugs cases*

In *R. v Green* [2009] EWCA Crim 1688; [2010] Crim. L.R. 306 CA the Court of **7–14** Appeal held that evidence that an accused's lifestyle involved the enjoyment of wealth beyond his apparent legitimate means was relevant to the question whether he had participated in a conspiracy to supply cocaine, and that it was not 'bad character' evidence the admissibility of which should have been regulated by the Criminal Justice Act 2003. It is, however, far from clear how this evidence, particularly that relating to the ownership of valuable property that had been purchased *before* the alleged conspiracy, tended to establish that the accused participated in such a conspiracy, *except* by tending to suggest that he had a general propensity to participate in some form of highly profitable, criminal activity. Perhaps there was scope to argue that the evidence was instead relevant as tending to demonstrate that the accused had the funds available to participate as a major player in a large conspiracy, but the Court did not identify this line of reasoning.

5.—WEIGHT OF EVIDENCE

7-18   In *R v Atkins and Atkins* [2009] EWCA Crim 1876; [2010] 1 Cr. App. R. 8 (p.117) considered whether a facial comparison expert could give evidence as to his opinion as to the weight that ought to be attached to his evidence that there were several similarities between the accused's facial features and those of the offender as captured by indistinct CCTV footage. The Court held that such an opinion was admissible, but discouraged any use of numbers in presenting it since this might erroneously suggest the existence of a measurable scale. In the subsequent case of *R. v T (footwear mark evidence)* [2010] EWCA Crim 2439; [2011] 1 Cr. App. R. 9 (p.85) a differently constituted Court of Appeal considered a case where an expert had provided an opinion as to the significance that ought to be attached to similarities between footwear marks found at the scene of a murder and the soles of a pair of Nike trainers owned by the accused. The Court confirmed that an expert's "evaluative opinion" was admissible, but insisted that such an opinion should not be derived by the use of "likelihood ratios or other mathematical formula" where there is no reliable database which records how frequently particular sole patterns and sizes are found and how they are distributed around society. (*R. v T (footwear mark evidence)* [2010] EWCA Crim 2439; [2011] 1 Cr. App. R. 9 (p. 85) is discussed further below, §15–05, §15–32 and §17–05.)

ATTENDANCE OF WITNESSES

2.—ATTENDANCE OF WITNESSES IN CIVIL CASES

(b) Requirements

(iv) Actual possession or custody

A recipient of a witness summons (or subpoena) is not obliged to bring documents **8–09** into his actual possession or custody for the purpose of bringing them to court. Thus, in *Dorojay Pty Ltd v. Aristocrat Leisure Ltd* [2006] FCA 333, (2007) 230 A.L.R. 549, the court found that documents held by foreign affiliate practices of the accounting firm PWC were not caught by a subpoena.

(v) Identification

The family courts are more relaxed in their approach in applying the requirement **8–10** of particular identification of documents. This doubtful approach has nonetheless been recognised by the courts in the context of letters of request: *Charman v. Charman* [2005] EWCA Civ 1606, [2006] 1 W.L.R. 1053; *SMSE v. KL* [2009] HKCA 349 at [36].

The requirement of particular identification of documents does not apply in the very different context of the FSA's statutory powers to investigate and assist a foreign regulator: *Financial Services Authority v. Amro* [2010] EWCA Civ 123, [2010] 3 All E.R. 723, CA.

(vi) Relevance and admissibility

In the context of the fact that the purpose of a witness summons or subpoena **8–11** is to bring evidence directly to the court, the Newfoundland and Labrador Court of Appeal in *Kent v. Kent* (2011) 324 D.L.R. (4th) 238 at [44–46] stated that a subpoena should not be used as a disguised form of discovery, but should focus on trial admissibility.

fn.33 A court is likely to set aside a witness summons (subpoena) seeking disclosure as to credit, as such documents would not go to the pleaded issues: *P&M Quality Smallgoods Pty Ltd v. Seven Network (Operations) Pty Ltd* [2010] NSWSC 841 at [17].

Where documents are sought for a pre-dominant improper or collateral purpose, a witness summons (subpoena) may be set aside: *Campaign Master v. Forty Two* [2010] FCA 398, (2010) 269 A.L.R. 7, Fed. Ct. of Australia. In Australia the courts have on occasion been willing to permit a subpoena for documents even where it is not sought for trial and do not go to any of the substantive or final issues in the action (contrary to the practice in England): *ASIC v. Rich* [2003] NSWSC 257 (to support an application for discovery against a party); *ACCC v. Pratt* (2009) 250 A.L.R. 663 (for purposes of an application to stay criminal proceedings as an abuse of process).

(d) *Procedure*

8–17   fn.68 *Waind v. Hill and National Employer's Mutual General Associated Ltd* [1978] 1 N.S.W.L.R. 372 (corrected citation).

3.—ATTENDANCE OF WITNESSES IN CRIMINAL CASES

(a) *Witness summonses*

8–26   The current rules are Criminal Procedure Rules 2011, Pt 28, which largely replicate the 2010 rules (as amended) in respect of witness summonses.

8–28   fn.121 Crim PR r.28.7(1)(c) (corrected citation).

(b) *Warrant*

8–31   fn.127 The procedure for dealing with a contempt in failing to comply with a witness summons under s.3 of the Criminal Procedure (Attendance of Witnesses) Act 1965 is now governed by Crim PR rr.62.5–62.8.

4.—WITNESSES WITHIN THE UNITED KINGDOM

8–32   fn.133 Whilst CPR r.71.2 does not enable an order for examination to be made against an officer of a corporate judgment debtor who is outside the jurisdiction (*Masri v. Consolidated Contractors International Company SaL* [2009] UKHL 43), this does not prevent an order being made against an officer who is temporarily within the jurisdiction. In such a case, care should be made before exercising such a jurisdiction against a foreigner: c.f. *Kuwait Airways v. Iraq Airways Corporation* [2010] EWCA Civ 740, where the Court of Appeal made an ex parte order against a foreign officer of a judgment debtor temporarily within the jurisdiction.

5.—WITNESSES OUT OF THE JURISDICTION

fn.153 However in the context of an incoming letter of request, the Supreme Court   **8–37**
of Bermuda was prepared to apply *Charman v. Charman* [2005] EWCA Civ 1606,
[2006] 1 W.L.R. 1053 and take a relaxed approach in the context of ancillary relief in
divorce proceedings to the requirement that documents should be specified: *Jennings*
v. Jennings [2009] Sup Ct (Ber) 62 at [18–19].

6.—EVIDENCE IN THE JURISDICTION FOR CIVIL PROCEEDINGS

(c) *No general disclosure of documents*

The requirement for the documents to be specified is relaxed in at least two fields.   **8–44**
First, in the context of ancillary relief applications in divorce proceedings, there is a
line of authority that the requirement to specify documents is relaxed. It is sufficient
given the quasi-inquisitorial role of the judge in ancillary relief litigation for the
request to refer to conjectural documents. *Jennings v. Jennings* [2009] SC (Bda) 62 at
[18–19] (incoming letter of request), applying *Charman v. Charman* [2006] 1 W.L.R.
1053, CA (outgoing letter of request). Secondly, so long as the classes of documents
are specified, it is not necessary for the FSA to specify particular documents when
seeking documents in aid of a foreign request required under s.171 of the Financial
Services and Markets Act 2000. *Financial Services Authority v. Amro* [2010] EWCA
Civ 123, CA.

7.—OBTAINING EVIDENCE OUT OF THE JURISDICTION OR FOR PROCEEDINGS ABROAD: CRIMINAL CASES

The Crown has a general duty of disclosure, which includes a duty to pursue all   **8–51**
reasonable lines of enquiry, whether these point towards or away from the suspect:
CPIA Code of Practice, para.3.5. The Attorney General's Guidelines (2005) and the
Code make it clear that the obligation of the Crown is to pursue reasonable lines of
enquiry in relation to material that may be held overseas, including states outside the
European Union. If it appears that there is relevant material, then the Crown should
take reasonable steps to obtain it, either informally or making use of the powers
contained in the Crime (International Co-operation) Act 2003 and international con-
ventions. The duty is to take reasonable steps as there are cases where a foreign court
for example will not compel production under a letter of request: *R. v. Flook* [2009]
EWCA Crim 682, [2010] 1 Cr. App. R. 30; see also *R. v. Alibhai* [2004] EWCA Crim
681, *R. v. Khyam* [2008] EWCA Crim 1612 at [37].

Whilst there are provisions for witnesses abroad to be able to give evidence for
trials in the UK by video-link, there is no provision which permits such evidence to
be given by telephone. Art.11(1) of the European Convention on Mutual Assistance
in Criminal Matters 2000 does provide for a request to be made for such evidence by
telephone, but that is subject to national law providing for evidence to be given in this
way: *R. v. Diane* [2009] EWCA Crim 1494, [2010] 2 Cr. App. R.1.

CHAPTER 9

COMPETENCE AND COMPELLABILITY, OATH AND AFFIRMATION

1.—COMPETENCE

(d) *Defective intellect*

R. (FB) v DPP also reported at [2009] 1 W.L.R. 2072.   **9–10**

(e) *Infancy*

In *Pease v R* [2009] NSWCCA 136 (see n.53), the New South Wales Court of   **9–11**
Criminal Appeal had rejected an appeal based on the trial judge's decision to allow a
child of six to give evidence unsworn. The case is briefly reported in the International
Journal of Evidence & Proof, Vol.13, No.4, p.360.

2.—COMPELLABILITY

The exemption under s.20 of the State Immunity Act 1978 also extends to the   **9–16**
private servants of the sovereign or head of State in question. Twenty Orders in
Council have been made under s.3 of the Consular Relations Act 1968. Three Orders
in Council have been made under s.12 of this 1968 Act with respect to Commonwealth
countries and the Republic of Ireland.

3.—COMPETENCE AND COMPELLABILTY IN CRIMINAL PROCEEDINGS OF DEFENDANTS AND THEIR SPOUSES

(b) *The wife or husband of the defendant*

Of course references to spouses, wives or husbands in statutory provisions on the   **9–21**
law of evidence now routinely refer instead to "spouse or civil partner" by reason of

[25]

the Civil Partnership Act 2004. Section 80 of the Police and Criminal Evidence Act 1984 is a case in point. This chapter should be read with this in mind.

(iii) *Compellability of the wife or husband of the defendant for the prosecution*

9–24   *R. v RL* also reported at [2009] 1 W.L.R. 626. For a useful discussion of the case and of the law relating to the compellability of spouses more generally, see 'A Criminal Defendant's Spouse as a Prosecution Witness' [2011] Crim.L.R. 613–626.

(iv) *Compellability of the wife or husband of the defendant for a co-defendant*

9–25   The Sex Discrimination Act 1975 has now been superseded by the Equality Act 2010.

4.—Oath and Affirmation

(c) *Forms of oath or affirmation*

(i) *Usual form*

9–30   The relevant paragraph remains 5.366 in *Stone's Justices' Manual 2011* (see n.167).

(v) *Other non-Christian forms*

9–34   *R. v Mehrban* endorsed in *R. v Majid* [2009] EWCA Crim 2563 at [19].

(d) *Who may administer oaths*

(i) *In England*

9–36   In para9.1 of CPR Part 32 PD ("Written Evidence"), the words in (2) are now omitted and in (4) the words "Senior Courts" have replaced "Supreme Court".[1] Administration of Justice Act 1985, s.65, and Courts and Legal Services Act 1990, s.113, both now repealed (see n.194).

---

[1] Commissioners for Oaths Act 1889 s.2 likewise amended (see n.195).

CHAPTER 10

EVIDENCE TAKEN OR SERVED BEFORE TRIAL: DUTY TO DISCLOSE EVIDENCE

1.—CIVIL CASES

(a) *Evidence taken before trial*

(ii) *Depositions*

After the sentence ending with fn.6: The order must state the date, time and place of the examination (CPR r34.8(5)). **10–03**

fn.13: The Court in *Barratt v Shaw & Ashton* [2001] EWCA Civ 137; [2001] C.P. Rep. 57 CA. described this rule as "a fallback procedure for when it seems preferable that the trial judge should hear some of the evidence orally."

(iii) *Witness statements and affidavits as evidence*

fn.23 See also *Barnes (t/a Pool Motors) v Seabrook & Ors* [2010] EWHC 1849 (Admin); [2010] CP Rep 42; [2010] ACD 87. **10–06**

fn.25 See also *West London Pipeline and Storage Ltd & Anor v Total UK Ltd & Ors [2008] EWHC 1729 (Comm)* which was concerned with the question of whether, at an interlocutory stage, the Court could order cross-examination of a person who has sworn an affidavit; the Court reviewed the case law concluding that ". . . the exercise of that power should be reserved for extreme cases where there is no alternative relief." (para.88.)

fn.26 Matthews and Malek, *Disclosure*, 4th edn (2012) Ch.16.

(v) *Expert reports*

A party who fails to disclose an expert's report may not use the report at the trial or call the expert to give evidence orally unless the court gives permission. (CPR r35.14. See also *Meredith & Anor v Colleys Valuation Services Ltd & Anor* [2001] EWCA Civ 1456.) **10–12**

2.—CRIMINAL CASES

(b) *Evidence taken or served before trial*

10–15   Chapter 21 of the Criminal Procedure Rules 2011 (S.I. 2011 / 1709), which came into force on October 3, 2011, entitled Initial Details Of The Prosecution Case, effectively reproduces the former Magistrates' Court (Advance Information) Rules 1985.

10–20   The relevant rules are now the Criminal Procedure Rules 2011 (S.I. 2011 / 1709).
10–21   The relevant rules are now the Criminal Procedure Rules 2011 (S.I. 2011 / 1709).
10–24   and fn.69 The relevant rules are now the Criminal Procedure Rules 2011 (S.I. 2011 / 1709).
10–28   The relevant rules are now the Criminal Procedure Rules 2011 (S.I. 2011 / 1709).
10–33   The relevant rules are now the Criminal Procedure Rules 2011 (S.I. 2011 / 1709).
10–38   The relevant rules are now the Criminal Procedure Rules 2011 (S.I. 2011 / 1709).
10–41   The relevant rules are now the Criminal Procedure Rules 2011 (S.I. 2011 / 1709).

(vi) *Principles relating to video-recorded evidence of children*

10–42   fn.108 replace with [2006] 2 Cr.App.R. 175 CA; [2006] EWCA Crim 472.

(d) *The duty to disclose evidence*

(i) *Historical background*

10–44   fn.126 See also *Fraser v Her Majesty's Advocate (Scotland)* [2011] UKSC 24.

(ii) *Common law rules on disclosure: Public interest immunity*

10–45   It is now rule 22.3 of the Criminal Procedure Rules 2011 which sets out the position governing applications by the prosecution to withhold disclosure on the grounds of public interest.

CHAPTER 11

RULES OF EVIDENCE RELATING TO THE COURSE OF A TRIAL: GENERAL

1.—CIVIL CASES

(7) *Proceedings in open court and in private*

In *JSC BTA Bank v Ablyazov* [2010] EWHC 545 (Comm)(QBD) interference with **11–10**
the public nature of court proceedings was necessary as an exception to the general
rule due to the particular circumstances of the case before the court. On the facts,
an order made pursuant to CPR r.39.2(3)(g), which withheld information from the
public regarding a receivership application, was deemed necessary (paras 32–35 per
Teare J).

2.—CRIMINAL CASES

(15) *The available special measures*   **11–36**

(a) *Screens*

The procedure for applying for a special measures direction is contained in Part 29
of the Criminal Procedure Rules 2011 (S.I. 2011 No.1709) which came into force on
October 3, 2011.

(b) *Live link*

It is impermissible to receive evidence in a criminal trial by telephone link, see *R v*   **11–37**
Diane [2010] 2 Cr. App. R. 1.

(e) *Video-recorded evidence in chief*

In *R v Popescu* [2010] EWCA Crim 1230; [2011] Crim. L. R. 227 it was restated   **11–40**
that it should only be for good reason that the jury should be given transcripts of
video-recorded evidence in chief during and after the witness had finished giving evidence and only in exceptional circumstances should they be allowed to retire with the

transcripts. Guidance was given on the appropriate procedure and jury directions in such circumstances.

(19) *Anonymity of witnesses*

11–49   The statutory provisions relating to anonymity orders from after December 31, 2009 are contained in the Coroners and Justice Act 2009 ss.86–97, Sch. 22 paras 16–22, following the repeal of the Criminal Evidence (Witness Anonymity) Act 2008 (save for ss.11–13 and 15).

For the procedure to be followed on an application for a witness anonymity order now see Consolidated Criminal Practice Direction (Amendment No. 24)(Criminal Proceedings; Witness Anonymity Orders (2) [2010] 2 Cr. App. R. 39; Criminal Procedure Rules 2011 Part 29.18 et seq.

There is no statutory or common law power to permit anonymous hearsay evidence to be read to the jury, see *R v Ford* [2010] EWCA Crim 2250; [2011] Crim. L. R. 475.

(20) *Absence of the defendant*

11–50   Counsel representing an absent defendant is entitled to conduct the trial by reference to instructions received both before and after the defendant absconded, see *R v Pomfrett* [2009] EWCA Crim 1939; [2010] 2 All E. R. 481; [2010] 1 W.L.R. 2567; [2010] Cri. App. R.28.

(30) *Recalling witnesses*

11–61   Whilst as a general rule a defendant should not be allowed to be recalled to contradict his earlier evidence (see *R v Ikram and Parveen* [2008] EWCA Crim 586; [2009] 1 W.L.R. 1419) there may be exceptional circumstances where it may be permissible to do so, see *R v Reid* [2010] EWCA Crim 1478; *Times,* July 19, 2010.

(33) *Court's duty to assist parties*

11–67   A magistrates' court's legal adviser has a duty to assist an unrepresented defendant, see Criminal Procedure Rules 2011, Part 37.14(3)

(38) *Submission of no case: test to be applied*

11–72   Where expert evidence cannot rule out a proposition consistent with innocence a court is nevertheless justified in leaving the case to the jury where on the evidence as a whole it would be safe to convict. In *R v Gian* [2009] EWCA Crim 2553; [2010] Crim LR 409 one of the issues was whether the victim had been killed or died from a cocaine overdose a cause which the expert did not accept but could not exclude as a theoretical possibility. The judge was upheld in rejecting a submission of no case.

(41) *Power of the judge to withdraw case from the jury at the end of the evidence*

A Crown Court judge has no power to quash a properly preferred indictment eg.   **11–75**
where he thought the expense of a trial was unjustified or a prosecution was without
merit, see *R v F.B., R v A.B; R v J.C.* [2010] EWCA Crim 1857. See also *R v SH* [2010]
EWCA Crim 1931.

(46) *Failure by the defendant to call evidence*

R v Khan [2001] All E. R. (D) 48; [2001] Crim. L . R. 673; [2001] EWCA Crim 486   **11–80**
was referred to and applied in *R v Campbell* [2009] EWCA Crim 1076; [2009] Crim
L. R. 822.

CHAPTER 12

RULES OF EVIDENCE RELATING TO THE COURSE OF A TRIAL: EXAMINATION OF WITNESSES

1.—CIVIL CASES

In *Cadogan Petroleum Plc v Tolley* [2009] EWHC 2527 (Ch D) the court affirmed its **12–02/12–11** discretionary power to allow cross-examination evidence to be used at trial, provided that all proceedings are dealt with in a just and expeditious manner. On the facts, the court made an order allowing the claimant to deploy evidence given in cross-examination only if the defendant elected to serve a witness statement in the action.

(5) *Anonymity of Witnesses*

In *A v Ward* [2010] EWHC 16, [2010] All ER (D) 2 (High Court of Justice Family **12–07** Division) Munby J held that professional witnesses cannot, either by general law or s.12 Administration of Justice Act 1960, be afforded anonymity. There could be no pressing need for such anonymity in relation to professional witnesses as the usual risks of being targeted, or suffering harassment or vilification could not alone out-weigh the powerful argument for denying such anonymity (see paras 144–155).

(9) *Cross-examination*

Re W (A Child) (Cross-examination) [2010] EWCA Civ 1449, [2011] 1 FLR 1979 **12–11** (Court of Appeal, Civil Division): the judge's decision to proceed with a hearing without providing a father, a litigant in person, the opportunity to cross-examine the guardian of his child in a case concerning contact arrangements between the father and child amounted to a procedural irregularity. The order made pursuant to the Children Act 1989, s.91(14), could not therefore stand.

2.—CRIMINAL CASES

(9) *Death or illness before cross-examination*

Where a prosecution witness is medically unfit to continue with cross-examination, **12–24** the overriding question is whether a fair trial is still possible. In *R v Lawless* [2011]

EWCA Crim 59; (2011) 175 J.P. 93, where the trial judge refused to discharge the jury when, after two hours of cross-examination, an important prosecution witness was medically unfit to continue giving evidence, his ruling was upheld on the basis that any prejudice was mitigated by a strong direction to the jury and that because the witness's evidence on a retrial would have been admitted under CJA 2003 s. 116 the defendant was no worse off.

The Court of Appeal decision in *R v Horncastle* [2009] EWCA Crim 964 has been upheld by the Supreme Court, [2010] UKSC 14; [2010] 2 A.C. 373; [2010] 1 Cr.App. R. 17; [2010] Crim LR 496. The Supreme Court decided that the CJA 2003 regime for admitting the evidence of an absent witness did not breach ECHR art. 6 and did not have to be disapplied in favour of the sole or decisive rule promulgated in *Al-Khawaja v United Kingdom* (2009) 49 E.H.R.R. 1; [2009] Crim LR 352 which decision itself has been referred by the UK Government to the Grand Chamber of the European Court of Human Rights whose decision is awaited after a hearing on May 19, 2010.

(28) *Examination by Judge*

12–43   Where the judge makes excessive interventions and is perceived as acting as a second prosecutor, indicating that he does not believe a word of what the defendant's evidence, an appellate court will quash the conviction no matter how obviously guilty the appellant, on the basis that there has not been a fair trial by an impartial judge; see *Michel v The Queen* [2009] UKPC 41 applying *Randall v The Queen* [2002 1 W.L.R. 2237 PC; [2002] 2 Crim App R 267.

For a case where the judge's rude, harsh and sarcastic conduct towards a defendant rendered the conviction unsafe see *R v Tedjame-Mortty* [2011] EWCA Crim 950. For a case where it was held that the judge's interventions did not render the trial unfair see *R v Zarezadeh* [2011] EWCA Crim 271; [2011] Crim LR 588.

(39) *Refreshing memory*

12–54   Whether or not the conditions in CJA 2003 s.139(1) have been met is a matter for the judge's discretion. He need not wait for the witness to stumble because of a faulty memory before permitting a witness to refresh his memory, see *R v Mangena* [2009] EWCA Crim 2535; (2010) 174 J.P. 67.

CHAPTER 13

EVIDENCE TAKEN AFTER TRIAL

1.—CIVIL CASES

(a) *New evidence after judgment but before order drawn up*

In *K v K (Abduction: Hague Convention: Adjournment)* [2009] EWHC 3378, [2010]   **13–01**
1 FLR 1310 where an administrative error had resulted in judgment being handed
down in ignorance of an application to admit fresh evidence, the test of 'strong
reasons or exceptional circumstances' set out in *Paulin v Paulin* [2009] EWCA Civ
221 had been satisfied so that the judgment, which had not yet been perfected, could
be reconsidered. Had the application have been made before judgment was given,
there would be no need to prove strong reasons per *M (Minors) (Abduction: Non-
Convention Country)* [1995] 1 FLR 89.

In *Sheikh v Dogan* [2009] EWHC 2935 (Ch D) the court refused to exercise the
jurisdiction in *Barrell Enterprises* [1973] 1 WLR 19 to reconsider the terms of an
extempore judgment before the relevant general civil restraint order was sealed, as
there were no strong reasons for doing so.

(b) *Further evidence on appeal: status of Ladd v Marshall*

In *Singh & Ors v Habib & ANR* [2011] EWCA Civ 599 the Court of Appeal (Civil   **13–06**
Division) held that *Ladd v Marshall* considerations, whilst important, "are not to be
taken as a straightjacket" (para.14), and it was in the public interest to admit fresh
evidence under CPR r.52.11(2) which raised concerns of fraud in relation to a road
traffic accident where damages were claimed for personal injury.

In *The Governing Body of St Andrew's Catholic Primary School v Blundell* [2011]
EWCA Civ 427, the Court of Appeal held that the *Ladd v Marshall* criteria, which
must be applied flexibly (para.30, per Elias LJ), were satisfied so as to permit admission of fresh evidence. Whilst the application for admission had been late (para.36),
the fresh evidence could materially influence the tribunal's factual assessments
which had constituted the basis of compensatory awards for unfair dismissal and
discrimination.

(c) *The* Ladd v Marshall *requirements*

(iii) *Credibility*

13–09   In *Jogo Associates Ltd v Internacionale Retail Ltd* [2011] EWCA Civ 384, fresh shareholder evidence was held to be inadmissible as it lacked credibility and failed to satisfy the conditions in *Ladd v Marshall* (paras 30–31). In contrast, the administrator's fresh evidence could be regarded as credible given that he was an officer of the court and had no financial interest in the dispute. As such, it was admissible since it could have a bearing on the outcome of the case.

In *R (Nyeko) v General Medical Council* [2011] EWHC 389 (Administrative Court), an application to admit fresh evidence was refused on the basis that the third criteria of credibility in *Ladd v Marshall* was unsatisfied. The appellant had sought to adduce fresh evidence that he was suffering from Post-traumatic stress disorder at the time of his medical misconduct. However, Mr Justice Cranston in the Administrative Court held that there was nothing to support this new case (para.41).

(iv) *Other factors not mentioned in* Ladd v Marshall

13–10   In *Noble v Owens* [2010] EWCA Civ 224, [2010] 1 WLR 2491, the Court of Appeal (Civil Division) held that where fresh evidence was adduced illustrating that the first instance judge had been deliberately misled, it could only order a retrial where fraud was admitted or evidence of it was incontrovertible. If the issue of fraud had to be tried in the absence of an admission, a fresh action need not be commenced and the issue could be referred under CPR r.52.10(2)(b) to a judge.

(d) *Application of* Ladd v Marshall *in particular types of appellate hearing*

13–11   [Whether *Ladd v Marshall* applies with equal validity to appeals to the Competition Appeal Tribunal] In *British Telecommunications Plc v Office of Communications* [2011] EWCA Civ 245 the Court of Appeal held that the question as to whether fresh evidence should be adduced on appeal to the Competition Appeal Tribunal was a matter for that tribunal to determine. Whilst the *Ladd v Marshall* criteria is of general application in civil appeals, an appeal to the CAT, pursuant to the Communications Act 2003, against a finding by OFCOM necessarily differs from ordinary civil claims since OFCOM does not ordinarily provide for witness cross-examination (para.69, per Lord Toulson). Therefore, CAT should:

"Adopt a more permissive approach towards the reception of fresh evidence than a court hearing an appeal from a judgment following the trial of a civil action" (para.70, per Lord Toulson).

As such, it is for the CAT to determine whether it is in the interests of justice in any given case for fresh evidence to be admitted, remembering that it is the responsibility of the party who wishes to introduce it to show good reasons for doing so (para.72, per Lord Toulson). No more specific guidance than this could be provided (ibid).

(g) *Reopening concluded appellate proceedings*

In *Guy v Barclays Bank Plc* [2010] EWCA Civ 1396, [2011] 1 WLR 681, the Court **13–17** of Appeal (Civil Division), applying *Re U (A Child)* [2005] EWCA Civ 52, held that it could not exercise its power under CPR r.52.17 to reopen a final determination of an appeal merely because that determination had been factually incorrect. Only where that decision had been made via corrupt processes, such as fraud or bias, could the final determination have been reopened (paras 29–40).

2.—CRIMINAL CASES

(b) *Evidence on appeal to the Court of Appeal (Criminal Division)*

(i) *Existing evidence*

It is not permissible to allow different psychiatrists to re-open, many years later, **13–19** an issue which was investigated and resolved at the time of trial. In *R v Evans* [2009] EWCA Crim 2243; [2010] Crim LR 491 permission to adduce evidence that the appellant was suffering from diminished responsibility at the time of the murder was refused where a thorough investigation had been carried out at the time of the killing by two reputable forensic psychiatrists.

(iii) *Evidence of matters occurring after the hearing*

The court will be mindful of the risk of a witness being manipulated after trial. For **13–26** an example of where fresh evidence was not received where it was being asserted by a witness that his evidence at trial was untrue see *R v Patel* [2010] EWCA Crim 1858.

CHAPTER 14

CORROBORATION, SUPPORTING EVIDENCE AND RELATED WARNINGS

2.—SITUATIONS WHERE SUPPORTING EVIDENCE IS REQUIRED BY STATUTE

(a) *Perjury Act 1911 section 13*

In *R. v Cooper* [2010] EWCA Crim 979, [2010] 2 Cr App R 13, [2010] 1 WLR 2390 **14–02** the accused had been tried for using a handheld mobile telephone whilst driving a heavy goods vehicle on May 12, 2008 and had testified that he had not done so, and had no reason to do so, since the cab of his vehicle had been fitted with a hands-free system. In support of this testimony he introduced a letter from a Halfords store stating that it had fitted the hands-free system on April 14, 2008. Later inquiries revealed that the deputy manager of the Halfords store had been uncertain as to the date when the system was fitted and had simply put in the letter the date which the accused told him was the date of fitting. The documentary records of the Halfords store revealed a "diary sheet" that stated the system had actually been fitted on July 25, 2008. The accused was subsequently convicted of perjury with respect to his testimony that the cab of his vehicle was fitted with a hands-free system at the time of the alleged offence. The evidence that his testimony on this point had been false comprised testimony from the deputy manager of the Halfords store and the "diary sheet". On appeal two questions arose with regard to the statutory requirement that a person cannot be convicted of perjury "solely upon the evidence of one witness as to the falsity of any statement alleged to be false". First, it was submitted by the Crown that this provision had no application whatsoever when evidence of falsity was provided by a "business document" admissible under an exception to the hearsay rule. Secondly, it was submitted that the statutory provision could be fulfilled by the admissible business document—the "diary sheet"—corroborating the testimony of the deputy manager. With regard to the first submission the Court of Appeal held that the statutory rule prohibits conviction where the only evidence of falsity is provided by business records which "depend on a single human source" (at [16]). Thus if one employee had recorded the date on which he did the work and another had recorded the date on which he took payment for the work being done then the accused could have been convicted, but in the particular case the "diary sheet" had been written solely by the deputy manager. On the second point, the "diary sheet" could not corroborate the deputy manager's testimony because it was not independent of his testimony: the deputy manager had only been able to testify to the date on which the work was done by referring to it, and it was only admissible as a "business document" because the deputy manager could testify as to its nature and significance.

3.—SITUATIONS WHERE A WARNING MAY BE NECESSARY

(a) *Types of witness*

(i) *Complainants in sexual cases*

14–06A   A body of research supports corroboration being sought where an adult complainant testifies to his or her memory of events which occurred when he or she was very young. Thus a Report by the Research Board of the British Psychological Society, *Guidelines on Memory and the Law*, (Leicester, revised version 2010) p.13 recommends, as a "rule of thumb" that:

> "All memories dating to the age of three years and below should be viewed with great caution and should not be accepted as memories without independent corroborating evidence".

Professor Adrian Keane has argued that there are compelling reasons for introducing a statutory requirement to this effect, whilst noting that what must be required must be something "other than corroboration in the strict sense, with its complex and highly technical rules": (A Keane, "The Use at Trial of Scientific Findings Relating to Human Memory" [2010] *Criminal Law Review* 19, at 29–30.) The same report also suggests (at p.13) that: where an adult gives evidence of "detailed and well-organised memories dating to events that occurred between 7 to 5 years of age" these "should be viewed with caution"; "detailed and well-organised memories dating to events that occurred between 5 to 3 years of age should be viewed with considerable caution"; and:

> "In general the accuracy of memories dating to below the age of about 7 years cannot be established in the absence of independent corroborating evidence."

The Court of Appeal, however, as shown by cases such as *R. v E* [2009] EWCA Crim 1370, has been unwilling to lay down any rule suggesting that a warning must ordinarily be given about the risk of relying on unsupported testimony of memories of events that occurred when the witness was very young.

(ii) *Accomplices*

14–07   *R. v Percival* [2010] EWCA Crim 1326 was an unusual case because the main prosecution witness in a murder trial was a "supergrass" who had previously been tried for the same murder, had pleaded guilty to conspiracy to pervert the course of public justice by supplying the appellant with a false alibi, and admitted having previously misled a court into reducing his sentence by manufacturing a false story of duress. The trial judge had warned the jury about the need for caution before relying on the testimony of such a witness, drawing attention to his character and the strong motives that he might have had for suggesting that someone other than himself was primarily responsible for the crimes concerned. In his appeal against his conviction, however, the appellant relied on the judge's failure to follow the guidance in *R. v B (MT)* [2000] Crim. L.R. 181 (discussed in *Phipson*, §14–06) to the effect that when a judge recommends that a jury should look for supporting material "he should identify the potentially supportive evidence". The Court of Appeal highlighted two matters in dismissing this ground of appeal. First, the Court pointed out that in *R. v B (MT)* it had been agreed that there was no independent evidence which supported the witness concerned, whilst in this case there was a complex web of evidence but particular concerns about how far it was reliable and how far it could be classed as supportive since the key witness may have known of much of it, as a result of his own previous trial for the murder, *before* he made his statements implicating the appellant. This meant that in *R. v B (MT)* the appropriate direction might have been relatively simple to formulate whilst in this case (at [98]):

> "If . . . the judge was to give a comprehensive direction on what was independently capable of supporting Alvin's evidence on the murder, it would have been a complex direction to have given, and was quite capable of going awry."

Secondly, the Court emphasized that in his discussion of each item of the evidence the judge had given clear guidance on the extent to which it might support the key witness's testimony if they felt able to attach weight to it. Whilst the Court of Appeal did not use the case as an occasion for expressly formulating guidance to future courts, in our opinion it usefully indicates that *R. v B (MT)* should not be read as requiring that whenever a judge gives a clear warning about the need to look for supporting material he or she must also provide a formal catalogue of the material that may be supportive: in some circumstances clear guidance about the potential usefulness of particular items of evidence may be both more appropriate and sufficient.

IDENTIFICATION

2.—VISUAL IDENTIFICATION

(a) *General Principle*

A new version of Code of Practice D has effect with regard to identification proce-   **15–03**
dures conducted after midnight on March 6, 2011.

(c) *Photographs and video films*

In *R. v Atkins and Atkins* [2009] EWCA Crim 1876; [2010] 1 Cr. App. R. 8 (p.117)   **15–05**
the Court of Appeal considered the admissibility of a facial comparison expert's
opinion as to the significance of his finding that there were several similarities between
the accused's face and the face of the offender as recorded on indistinct CCTV
footage: the expert's testimony was that the similarities offered:

> "a level of support for the allegation that [the accused] and the offender are one
> and the same person, between 'it lends support' and 'lends strong support' to that
> conclusion."

The Court of Appeal held that such an opinion was admissible, despite the absence
of any statistical database recording the frequency with which the particular similar
facial features appear in the population at large. The Court also suggested, however,
that where such opinions are presented with reference to a verbal hierarchy (no
support, limited support, moderate support, etc.) no numbers should be used to refer
to the different levels since to do so might carry the risk of the jury concluding that
there was a measurable scale. Moreover, the Court stated that an expert offering such
an opinion would "plainly need to be asked" in cross-examination:

> "How, if no-one knows how often ears or noses of the shape relied upon appear in
> the population at large, it is possible to say anything at all about the significance of
> the match"

and commended the trial judge's directions, which had made clear that the expert's
opinion as to the significance of the similarities was "informed by experience but

entirely subjective" (at [29]-[31]). (*R. v Atkins and Atkins* [2009] EWCA Crim 1876; [2010] 1 Cr. App. R. 8 (p.117) was considered by a differently constituted Court of Appeal in the important subsequent case of *R. v T (footwear mark evidence)* [2010] EWCA Crim 2439; [2011] 1 Cr. App. R. 9 (p.85). In this case the Court accepted that an expert opinion such as that offered in *Atkins and Atkins* was admissible, but emphasized that it should not be derived from "likelihood ratios or other mathematical formula" and should be presented without the use of the word "scientific" (at [93]-[96]). *R. v T (footwear mark evidence)* [2010] EWCA Crim 2439; [2011] 1 Cr. App. R. 9 (p.85) is discussed further above §15–05, §15–32 and §17–18.)

In *R. v Moss* [2011] EWCA Crim 252 the Court of Appeal distinguished *R. v Smith (Dean Martin)* [2008] EWCA Crim 1342; [2009] 1 Cr.App.R. 36 CA. In *Moss* an off-duty police officer had identified the accused from a CCTV image that he saw over a colleague's shoulder whilst visiting the police station to check his e-mail. He only recorded this identification in his pocket book when he returned to duty a week later, and did not make a detailed statement recording how he recognised the accused until six months later. The Court of Appeal suggested that the guidance given in *Smith* was obviously appropriate where the police were conducting a "relatively formal procedure", such as police officers being shown CCTV films in order to make an identification, but:

> "It is necessary to appreciate, however, that what is required is not so much slavish adherence to a procedure but evidence that enables the jury to assess the reliability of the evidence of recognition, however it is provided" (at [20]).

In the circumstances it seems that the jury were sufficiently well-placed to assess the reliability of the evidence because there were some records of how the police officer made his identification and the CCTV film itself was available for the jury.

(d) *Protection against weak and unfair identification evidence*

(ii) *Excluding identification evidence under Police and Criminal Evidence Act 1984 section 78*

15–08   A new version of Code of Practice D has effect with regard to identification procedures conducted after midnight on March 6, 2011. The original text of the *Phipson on Evidence* 17th edn refers to the version of Code D that came into force on February 1, 2008. Below we list the references to the provisions of Code D (2011 version) which correspond to the references in the original text to Code D (2008 version), but in all cases except one both the numbering and wording of the relevant provisions in the 2011 version are the same as those of the provisions referred to in the original text.

(iii) *Important elements of fair identification procedure*

15–09   fn.101 Code D (2011) 3.1.
fn.102 Code D (2011) 3.2(a).
fn.102 Code D (2011) 3.2(a).
fn.104 Code D (2011) 3.1.

15–11   The relevant wording of Code D (2011) 3.12 is identical to the wording of Code D (2008) 3.12.

fn.109 Code D (2011) 3.4. The definition is unchanged.
fn.110 Code D (2011) 3.12 and 3.13.
fn.116 Code D (2011) 3.2(d) is worded differently from Code D (2008) 3.2(d), which is discussed in footnote. The 2011 wording:

> "Once there is sufficient information to justify the arrest of a particular individual for suspected involvement in the offence, e.g., after a witness makes a positive identification, the provisions [for obtaining identifications of known and available suspects] shall apply for any other witnesses in relation to that individual"

makes no express statement about when, if ever, a witness who has made a positive 'street identification' may have to attempt subsequently to identify a suspect in a formal identification procedure.
fn.120 Code D (2011) 3.14 and 3.16.

fn.121 Code D (2011) 3.21.   **15–12**
fn.122 Code D (2011) 3.23.

fn.125 Code D (2011) 3.4. The definition of a "known" suspect is unchanged.   **15–13**
fn.126 Code D (2011) 3.2 and Annex E (2011).
fn.127 Code D (2001), Annex E, para.6.

3.—DIRECTIONS ON VISUAL IDENTIFICATION EVIDENCE

(a) Turnball warnings

(ii) Cases where the defence alleges fabrication

In Grieves v R [2011] UKPC 39, the appellant argued that the judge had failed,   **15-19**
inter alia, adequately in summing up, to deal with the inconsistency between W's evidence about the firearms and the ballistics evidence, and the inconsistency in W and R's evidence. The appeal was dismissed, the court holding that *Turnbull* required the judge to remind the jury of any specific weaknesses which appeared in the identification evidence – it did not require the judge to remind the jury generally of every argument there may be for not believing a witness (see para.34 of the judgement).

(e) Code D warnings

In *R. v Gojra; R. v Dhir* [2010] EWCA Crim 1939; [2011] Crim. L.R. 311 CA the   **15-30**
Court of Appeal held that Code D had been broken as a result of a failure to require one of two victims of a crime to attempt formal identification of one of the suspects, Gojra, and his appeal against conviction was allowed because the judge had not given a "clear and unequivocal" direction about the "possible prejudice" resulting from this breach. The case was unusual, however, since the prosecution did not rely on any evidence of identification from this victim. Thus the Court of Appeal must have envisaged that the judge ought to have directed the jury that when assessing the weight of the identification evidence from other witnesses, including one of the victims and two co-accused, they should bear in mind that a breach of the Code had

deprived Gojra of the possibility of showing that he could not be formally identified by the other victim.

4.—OTHER MEANS OF IDENTIFICATION

(a) *Fingerprints, footmarks and similar body impressions*

15–32   The main issue in *R. v T (footwear mark evidence)* [2010] EWCA Crim 2439; [2011] 1 Cr. App. R. 9 (p.85) concerned whether an expert could provide an opinion derived from a "likelihood ratio" as to the weight which ought to be attached to his finding of similarities between a footwear mark at a crime scene and a pair of Nike trainers owned by the accused. (This aspect of the case is discussed further above, §7–18 and §15–05.) In passing, however, the Court of Appeal made reference (at [65]–[66]) to a distinction, which appears to be useful, between characteristics which only tend to show that a footwear mark was made by a pair of shoes of a particular size and brand ("class characteristics") and characteristics, such as an unusual pattern of wear or damage, that tend to show that a footwear mark was made by a particular pair of shoes ("identifying characteristics").

fn.216 The opinion expressed by the Court of Appeal in *R. v Gray (Paul Edward)* [2003] EWCA Crim 1001 has now been overtaken by the decision in *R. v Atkins and Atkins* [2009] EWCA Crim 1876; [2010] 1 Cr. App. R. 8 (p.117), discussed above, §15–05.

fn.222 Code of Practice D (2011), Pt 4.

fn.226 Code of Practice D (2011), Pt 6.

(c) *Voice recognition*

(ii) *Lay listener evidence*

15–35   *R. v Flynn* [2008] EWCA Crim 970; [2008] 2 Cr.App.R. 20 CA, was considered by the Court of Appeal in *R. v Miah and Hussain* [2010] EWCA Crim 2638. In this case the trial judge had admitted testimony from two translators that particular statements recorded by a bugging device were uttered by the same speaker as other statements; the prosecution had then relied on other evidence to identify the speakers. The translators were not experts in voice recognition, and the prosecution had not instructed an expert to give an independent opinion on the validity of their attributions, apparently because it was believed that no expert was unavailable who could speak the languages that the speakers used. It was accepted that the recordings were of good quality and the translators had been provided with sufficient material for comparative purposes. The Court of Appeal held that in these circumstances, particularly since other attributions of the translators had been proved correct by admissions in the case, the trial judge had been correct to admit the testimony, and any shortfall with regard to keeping records of the processes that led to the translators reaching their conclusions went only to the weight of their evidence.

CHARACTER—GENERAL AND INTRODUCTORY

3.—DIRECT ISSUE CASES

(a) *Civil cases*

p.[477], The first "claimant" should read "defendant". (Correction).   **17–04**

fn.13 The principles stated in *Burstein v Times Newspapers Ltd* and *Turner v News Group Newspapers Ltd* were applied in *Kaschke v Gray and Hilton* [2010] EWHC 1907 (QB). However, in *Hunt v Evening Standard Ltd.* [2011] EWHC 272 (QB), Tugendhat J. suggested that the scope of the principle that evidence of a claimant's reputation is admissible in mitigation of damage was unclear, perhaps because in a stage of development (see at [28]).

fn.14 *Warren v The Random House Group Ltd* was followed in the Northern Irish case of *O'Rawe v William Trimble Ltd.* [2010] NIQB 135.

(b) *Criminal cases*

The House of Lords, in *R. v JTB* [2009] UKHL 20; [2009] A.C. 1310, held that the   **17–07** enactment of s.34 of the Crime and Disorder Act 1998 had resulted in the abolition, not just of the presumption of doli incapax, but of the very doctrine itself. However, in R v H [2010] EWCA Crim 312, the court confirmed that the doctrine still applies to offences alleged to have been committed prior to the coming into force, eg. s.34. As a result, the precise matter discussed in the text only apply to offences alleged to have been committed prior to September 30, 1998, though the authorities remain instructive on the important distinction between cases in which character is raised as a direct issue, and cases in which it is not.

CHAPTER 18

GOOD CHARACTER

1.—GOOD CHARACTER OF THE ACCUSED

(e) *The judicial direction on good character*

The courts have continued to work out the precise requirements for the form of the **18–12** direction. The tendency of the most recent authority is to indicate that, not only is it insufficient for the judge to tell the jury that the accused is *entitled to argue* that they should take good character into account, as held in *R. v Moustakim* [2008] EWCA Crim 3096 (see *R. v Gbajabiamila* [2011] EWCA Crim 734), but, more strongly, as held in *R. v CM* [2009] EWCA Crim 158; [2009] 2 Cr.App.R. 54, that the judge is to direct the jury that they must, rather than that they are entitled to, take good character into account. To this effect are *R. v Anadu* [2010] EWCA Crim 532; *R. v Remice* [2010] EWCA Crim 1952; *R. v Feeley* [2010] EWCA Crim 1836; *R. v BS* [2010] EWCA Crim 2691; and *R. v Hall* [2011] EWCA Crim 159, though, in both *R. v Joseph* [2010] EWCA Crim 2580 and *R. v Yee-Mon* [2011] EWCA Crim 1069, the entitlement formula was found sufficient.

Whilst the appeal courts maintain that it is not essential for the judge slavishly to follow the relevant Judicial Studies Board Specimen Direction on good character (now 4.8), there are growing signs, in the cases cited in the previous paragraph (and also in *R. v Omolewa and Grant-Daley* [2011] EWCA Crim 412), of a lack of tolerance of departure there from. That said, there continues to be appellate understanding of a lack of absolute clarity of language, as well as of slips of the tongue—see *R. v Joseph* and *R. v Yee-Mon*, above, but also, in particular, *R. v Tut* [2010] EWCA Crim 1878.

fn.52 In *R. v Campbell* [2010] UKPC 26; [2011] 2 W.L.R. 983, where the failure **18–13** of defence counsel to rely upon the good character of his client seems clearly to have arisen from the most gross incompetence upon counsel's part, the case against Campbell, that he had murdered a police officer had relied, in essence, on the identification of him, as the perpetrator, by one witness. In those circumstances, the Privy Council, in advising Her Majesty to remit the case to the local appeal court, with a direction to quash the verdict of guilty, pointed out that, Campbell having given evidence denying any involvement:

"[t]he absence of a good character direction . . . deprived [Campbell] of a benefit in precisely the kind of case where such a direction must be regarded as being of greatest potential significance" (at para.45, per Lord Mance).

(ii) *The "second limb" direction*

18–16   An interesting point arises from "historic sex abuse" cases. Thus, in *R. v GJB* [2011] EWCA Crim 867, the charges concerned sexual offences that had allegedly taken place almost twenty years before, yet there was no evidence of the accused having committed a sexual offence, or, indeed, any offence, in the intervening years. In those circumstances, the court held that it had been incumbent upon the trial judge to give what amounted to an additional, "third limb" direction, that the fact that the accused had:

> "not committed any offence, let alone one involving sexual abuse, since the date of the alleged offence goes to the likelihood or otherwise of his having committed the offence." (see para.[18], per Stanley Burnton L.J.) – cf. the first note, below, to para.18.20.

(iii) *Co-accused of good and bad characte*

18–17   *R. v Bashier and Razak* [2009] EWCA Crim 2003 raises a rather different issue with regard to co-accused of good and bad character. There, Bashier had spent convictions for offences of dishonesty, whilst two co-accused had no convictions at all. The court thought it right for the trial judge to take account of the need for fairness to them, in deciding not to give a full good character direction, as regards Bashier, despite the spent status of his convictions. By contrast, in *R. v Miller and Frisby* [2010] EWCA Crim 3136, where the co-accused Miller and Usher, had mounted cut-throat defences with regard to an alleged conspiracy to defraud, the court considered not unfair a direction encouraging the jury not to take account of Usher's admission to the (separate) theft of £10,000 from the very company involved in the alleged fraud, as going either to the issue or to Usher's credibility. It must be reiterated that this kind of issue, involving the competing interests of co-accused is one of the greatest difficulty.

(f) *"Good character" for the purposes of the direction*

18-18   fn.70 See *R v Garien* [2011] EWCA Crim (no transcript available yet), where the Court of Appeal held that the judges direction that E's good character could be used to his advantage was inadequate. The words used had to be affirmative and definitive – the phrase "could be used" diluted the direction.

fn.73 A recent example of the court refusing to have its common sense offended is *R. v Hasanali* [2009] EWCA Crim 1558.

fnn.76 and 77 The reasoning in *R. v Martin* was refined in *R. v Despaigne-Pellon* [2009] EWCA Crim 2580 and in *R. v Mazekelua and another* [2011] EWCA Crim 1458. Thus, in the latter case, though it was stated that, in these circumstances, the extent to which such a direction is given lies within the *discretion* of the trial judge (as had been remarked in *R. v Lodge* [2009] EWCA Crim 2651), the court emphasised that the first limb direction *must* be given where the offence(s) giving rise to the caution(s) has/have no adverse impact at all upon the credibility of the accused. The same must, presumably, apply to the second limb (propensity) direction, where there is no impact on the issue.

(i) *The convicted accused*

fn.80 *R. v Gray* was followed in *R. v Baquari* [2010] EWCA Crim 1279, where the charges were of sexual assault, the conviction one for failing to provide a breath specimen for analysis.   **18–19**

An important point that has emerged from some of the cases concerned with allegations of historic sexual and/or other abuse of children is that misconduct of the accused that is of considerable antiquity may be relevant to the issue, precisely because it took place within a period of time reasonably close to the matters presently alleged against the accused, so demonstrating a relevant propensity of the accused at that time. In *R. v BS* [2010] EWCA Crim 2691 (considered in detail below, in the penultimate note to para.18–21), the misconduct did not entail criminality, but the point is capable of applying no less to old crimes, whether or not resulting in conviction. On the other hand, where the misconduct is accounted relevant to credibility, this point should not apply, since it must be the accused's credit, whether with regard to his present testimony, or to other admissible evidence of something said by him, *at the time of trial* that counts.   **18–20**

fn.86 In *R. v Bashier and Razak* [2009] EWCA Crim 2003, the court affirmed the trial judge's decision not to give a full good character direction where the charge was one of conspiracy to produce cannabis, and the spent convictions were for offences of dishonesty, though it is to be observed that the accused there had put himself forward as an "honest and hard working businessman" (see para. [43]).

fn.91 As pointed out in the note to para.18–12 above, the most recent cases tend to prefer the approach taken in *R. v CM* to that taken in *R. v MW*.

(ii) *The unconvicted accused*

Where the trial judge *does* decide that the unconvicted accused should not enjoy the benefit of any element of the good character direction, it is not open to him to give no jury direction at all about character. Rather, the jury should, as was held in *R. v Lodge* [2009] EWCA Crim 2651, be given the conventional guidance about bad character (on which, see the text, at paras 19–57—19–58, 20–21, 20–38, and 21–13—21–15).   **18–21**

fn.94 In *R. v Hamer* [2010] EWCA Crim 2053; [2011] 1 W.L.R. 528; [2011] 1 Cr.App.R. 23, it was held that, unlike a caution, which involves the person cautioned acknowledging their guilt, a fixed penalty notice involves no such acknowledgment. Therefore, the notice itself does not constitute evidence of bad character, though, of course, if evidence of the underlying conduct itself be given, that might well do.

fnn.101 and 102 *R. v Gray* is often cited in the most recent authorities, usually with regard to the tightness of appellate control of trial judge exercise of the residual discretion not to give a direction, as in *R. v Webb* [2011] EWCA Crim 1270, but sometimes as not denying the fact sensitive nature of that discretion, as in *R. v Joseph* [2010] EWCA Crim 2580.

fnn.104 and 105 In the interesting case of *R. v BS* [2010] EWCA Crim 2691, the accused's convictions, which were for minor and spent offences of dishonesty, had been treated by the trial judge as detracting from his good character, in a case where the charges themselves concerned allegations of (historic) sexual and violent abuse of his children and stepchildren. The court clearly thought that the judge had been wrong so to treat them, but found his convictions not to be unsafe. Its reason for doing so was that the accused had admitted, in evidence, that, when in his late thirties, he had had a full sexual relationship with a step-daughter, by then aged 16, who was one of the (sexual) complainants. As the court pointed out, this was reprehensible conduct, showing a propensity to abuse his position as stepfather, so would have been relevant evidence of bad character, for that reason, yet the judge had not referred to it, in directing the jury. So, in effect, had he done so, the accused would have appeared to the jury in a much more unfavourable light than that cast by minor dishonesty convictions. The clear implication is that non-criminal conduct can indeed be taken into account in the judicial directions.

In *R. v Olu, Wilson and Brooks* [2010] EWCA Crim 2975; [2011] 1 Cr.App.R. 404, Olu denied the commission of an offence for which he had received a police caution. Having made the point that it might equally be possible for an accused to challenge a conviction (citing *R. v O'Dowd* [2009] EWCA Crim 905; [2009] 2 Cr.App.R. 280), the court ruled that the correct course for the trial judge to take was to direct the jury on the alternative hypotheses that they did, and that they did not, find the extraneous offence to have been committed. Thus, Olu should have enjoyed (though he had not) the advantage of what would, in effect, have been a conditional good character direction.

2.—GOOD CHARACTER OF OTHERS

(a) *Relevance to a fact in issue*

(i) *Criminal cases*

18–23   fn.110 Further, implicit support for the position taken in the text is to be found in *R. v Higgins and Guy* [2010] EWCA Crim 308, at [45]. Explicit support for it is to be found in *R. v Q* [2011] EWCA Crim 1824, where, the court made specific reference to the statement of Maurice Kay L.J. in *R. v Ali*, to that effect (see, further, below at para.18–24)

18–24   In *R. v Q* [2011] EWCA Crim 1824, the accused alleged that the assault occasioning actual bodily harm to a child with which he stood charged had, in fact, been carried out by a prosecution witness and a third party. Indeed, he had attacked their characters, not just by virtue of that allegation, but also by reference to their alleged extraneous violence towards other children. The court held that the trial judge had been right, not only in allowing him to be cross-examined about his convictions, but also in allowing the prosecution to call, in rebuttal, evidence that neither the witness nor the third party had, themselves, any convictions. The latter element of evidence was clearly held to be admissible on the basis of its relevance to the issue of who was responsible for the assault now charged.

(b) *Relevance to credibility*

18–26   fn.125 In *R v E* [2011] EWCA Crim 1690, the court admitted the evidence of a consultant psychologist, rejecting the argument of the defence that it was a form of oath helping, on the basis that it was relevant material for the jury to take into account in determining where the truth lay.

CHAPTER 19

BAD CHARACTER OF THE ACCUSED (PROSECUTION ASPECTS)

1.—INTRODUCTION TO ACCUSED'S BAD CHARACTER

19–02 fn.10 That the sentiments expressed by Sir Igor Judge P. (as he then was) in *R. v Renda* have not resulted in the stemming of the flow of cases to the Court of Appeal (Criminal Division) is demonstrated by the fact that a series of LEXIS searches revealed that over 100 cases had been decided, during the two-year period between completion of work for the 17th. edition and work being done for this Supplement, on the various aspects of the statutory regime.

fn.12 Appeal courts continue to stress that a considerable degree of autonomy is granted to the trial judge. Good recent examples are *R. v Tye* [2009] EWCA Crim 1738, at [20] and *R. v Harris* [2011] EWCA Crim 912, where it was stated that the appeal court would interfere only where, "the judge's ruling is clearly outside the parameters of his judgment and discretion" (see at [14], per H.H. Judge Gordon).

fn.16 *R. v Murphy* was applied in *R. v McGarvie* [2011] EWCA Crim 1414.

3.—THE COMMON LAW

(a) *Introduction*

19–05 fn.24 For discussion of the most recent cases suggesting that, where, in the view of the court, the disposition mode of reasoning is not being relied upon by the proponent, the case for admission of the evidence in question is stronger, see the notes below, to paras 19–26 and 19–27.

4.—CRIMINAL JUSTICE ACT 2003

(b) *The scope of the Act*

19–11 In *R. v Creed* [2011] EWCA Crim 144 (see, also, *R. v McKenzie* [2011] EWCA Crim 1550), the point raised was whether or not the relevant provisions of the 2003 Act should be employed in proceedings, under s.4A of the Criminal Procedure (Insanity) Act 1964 (as amended), by which a jury must determine if the accused did the act, or made the omission, constituting the factual element of the crime charged, prior to the issue of unfitness to plead being determined. It was held that they should, either because those proceedings constitute "criminal proceedings", as defined in s.112(1) of the 2003 Act itself, or because, though they do not, the court should adopt the same rules of evidence for them. The case follows *R. v Chal* [2008] 1 Cr.App.R. 247; [2007] EWCA Crim 2647, which has the same effect, as regards the hearsay provisions of the 2003 Act, and is referred to at fn.324 to the text at para.28–52.

(c) *The gateways of admissibility*

19–12   fnn.50 and 51 Another case combining an emphasis upon the importance of the parties complying with the notice provisions with a refusal to interfere with the trial judge's decision to allow in the evidence nonetheless, is *R. v Ramirez* [2009] EWCA Crim 1721.

19–14   *As both R. v Cundell* (referred to in fn.47a of the text) and *R. v Marsh* [2009] EWCA Crim 2696 hold, *R. v Highton* applies no less to cases where the evidence was originally admitted through gateway (a) (agreement of the parties), than to those where it was admitted through some other gateway.

(d) *Res gestae and connected cases (common law)*

(i) *Res gestae cases proper*

19–16   A recent case with some similarity to *R. v Cobden* is *R. v Bevan* [2010] EWCA Crim 2324, where it was held that the evidence in question did "have to do with" the facts of the offence charged. For the details of this case, see para. 19–21 below.

(v) *After the 2003 Act*

19–21   The appropriate meaning to be given to the phrase "has to do with" has continued to create difficulty in the cases. In general, the courts have tended towards an interpretation of that phrase that is close to the core concept of res gestae at common law, i.e. restricting the phrase such that it covers only cases described, in the text, as "res gestae cases proper", though with rather more emphasis than under to common law upon the importance of at least approximate contemporaneity, and rather less emphasis upon that of close factual connection. Given the difficulty of the law here, it is worth setting out some examples, in detail.

The most straightforward case is *V.O.S.A. v Ace Crane and Transport Ltd.* [2010] EWHC 288 (Admin). There, it was held that, on a charge against an employer of permitting his driver to fail to keep proper records under provisions of the Transport Act 1968, it was permissible for the prosecution to adduce evidence of the employer's earlier contraventions. This was because the actus reus of the present offence was capable of being proved by evidence of the employer's systematic failure to perform his duty, which, in consequence had to do with the facts of the offence charged.

In *R. v Loftus and Comben* [2009] EWCA Crim 2688, Loftus was accused of the sexual abuse of two of Comben's children, Comben herself of neglect of them by failing to do anything, on a specific occasion when she was present, to prevent such abuse. The court ruled that the phrase did not embrace evidence of Loftus compelling Comben, on other occasions, to engage with him in sexual practices to which she objected, which she sought to adduce to explain her failure to intervene on the occasion at issue. The court went on to hold that the evidence was clearly admissible for her through gateway (e) (on which point, see para.21–04 below). In *R. v Brand* [2009] EWCA Crim 2878, the accused was alleged to have raped the complainant just outside his car, then, when she sought to get back into the car, where, according to her, her handbag was located, had pushed her away and driven off. At a first trial, for theft of the handbag, his defence was that it had always been in her possession, but he was convicted. At a second trial, for the alleged rape, the judge allowed evidence to be given, of that conviction, apparently as "bad character evidence", but the appeal court ruled that it fell clearly within s.98(a). That evidence, unlike that in *Loftus and Comben*, would surely have counted as res gestae at common law, since it amounted to part of the transaction under review. Similarly, in *R. v McPherson* [2010] EWCA Crim 2906, the violence against his wife and stepdaughters, with which the accused was charged, was said to have immediately followed, and arisen out of, an alleged rape of the wife. A rather more extended view of factual connection was taken in *R. v Bevan* [2010] EWCA Crim 2324, though one not inconsistent with the common law authorities (see, in particular, *R. v Cobden*, dealt with in the text at para.19–16). There, the evidence was from a CCTV camera, showing that, shortly before the accused had allegedly attempted to rob the complainant at knifepoint, he and his co-accused had been trying to break into a series of cars. As Laws L.J. put it (at [8]), "the events recorded were part and parcel of the overall circumstances of the offence".

To be contrasted with these relatively straightforward cases might seem to be *R. v O, C and D* [2010] EWCA Crim 1336. There, the prosecution case was that a knife had been produced, leading the complainant to submit to rape. The trial judge treated evidence that, some four days later, the accused C had been carrying a (different) knife as caught by s.98(a), though she went on to say that it was also admissible under s.101(1)(d). In upholding her decision about admissibility, the court did not make it clear whether or not it supported both of her grounds, though its language tends to suggest that it had the s.101(1)(d) ground in mind, and that certainly seems the much more persuasive basis for admission.

Finally, in the very important case of *R. v Mullings* [2011] 2 Cr.App.R. 21;[2010] EWCA Crim 2820, the court discussed many of the leading cases to date. There, the prosecution had been permitted to call evidence of the accused's possession of certain documents indicative of support of one Manchester gang, and antipathy towards another, to advance its case that the accused, when part of a group containing members of the former gang, which was confronting those of the latter gang, must have been aware that others in the group were carrying firearms with intent to endanger life, and must have shared that intent. The court had no doubt that that evidence, though admissible under s.101(1)(d), did not "have to do with" the alleged facts of the offence. It was the absence of any close temporal connection that led it to that conclusion (see also *R. Yaqoob* [2010] EWCA Crim 2817, which is to similar effect). An example that the court gave of evidence that would satisfy s.98(a) is instructive (see at [31]). It envisaged evidence that the accused might, at the very time of the confrontation, have been shouting out similar sentiments of support and antipathy. Though, on such a supposition, the temporal connection would undoubtedly be shown, it seems clear enough that the factual one would too, with the result that the shouting would properly have been accounted part of the transaction under review, at common law.

Furthermore, the court added the very important point that, "[t]he wider s.98(a) is construed, and the wider the embrace of evidence which 'has to do' with the facts of the alleged offence, the less effective the statutory purpose becomes", with the consequence that, "the narrower view of s.98(a) is to be preferred" (see at [32], per Pitchford L.J.) It is submitted that this reasoning is wholly convincing. (*Mullings* was applied in *R. v Hewgill, Hancock and Murray* [2011] EWCA Crim 1775).

Mullings also rejects a novel point about s.98(a) that had been made in *R. v Fox* [2009] EWCA Crim 653. In that case, the court had held that the phrase "has to do with the alleged facts" contemplated only the factual elements of the alleged offence, so not any element of mens rea, with the result that evidence of other events that tended to suggest that the accused would have had a sexual *purpose* when taking photographs of two seven-year-old girls was not caught by that phrase. Supporting Ormerod's critical commentary on this aspect of *Fox* at [2009] Crim.L.R. 881, the court in *Mullings* refused to accord s.98(a) such a narrow meaning.

In the text, it was envisaged that, for the purposes of s.98(b), any "misconduct in connection with the investigation or prosecution" of an offence would be that either of the police or of the accused, and those two possibilities were certainly the only ones in the mind of the Law Commission, in recommending enactment of such a provision. However, in *R. v Scott* [2009] EWCA Crim 2457, it had been argued for the accused, at trial, that there was no need to seek leave (under s.100 of the 2003 Act) to call evidence from a friend of the accused that the complainant (of rape) had sought to intimidate that friend into believing that the accused really had raped her, nor to seek leave then to cross-examine the complainant about that allegation. The basis for counsel's argument was that such evidence was caught by s.98(b), but the judge's decision to reject that argument was upheld on appeal, because, "[t]he misconduct has to have some closer link with the actual investigation of the offences or with their actual prosecution" (see at [38], per Aikens L.J.). However, *Scott* was distinguished in *R. v Apabhai, Apabhai and Amani* [2011] EWCA Crim 917. There, one of the Apabhais alleged that Amani had given him seven days to pay Amani £125,000, in return for Amani not changing his statement to the investigating customs officers such as to place all of the blame for the (fraud) offences at hand upon Apabhai. The appeal court upheld the judge's decision that that evidence was caught by s.98(b). Of course, the alleged misconduct here was that of an accused person, though the issue to which it related was not one between that accused and the prosecution, which is what the Law Commission might be thought to have had wholly in mind. It remains to be seen whether there will be circumstances in which the courts will be prepared to extend the ambit of s.98(b) to misconduct by a complainant or other third party.

19–22   The text ought to make it clear that the s.78(1) discretion is, in any event, available only as against the prosecution, so not, for example, in a case where an accused is seeking to adduce evidence against a co-accused, as in *Apabhai, Apabhai and Amani* (dealt with in the preceding paragraph).

(e) *Important explanatory evidence*

19–23   It continues to be vital to realise that the appropriate width of the s.101(1)(c) gateway for important explanatory evidence is closely connected with the meaning of "has to do with" in s.98(a), which has just been discussed. In this respect, there are now good grounds for believing that the line between the two provisions is drawn (to use the phraseology of the text at para.19–20) between "res gestae cases proper" (embraced by s.98(a)), and "connected cases" (dealt with by s.101(1)(c)). So, not only does *R. v Pronick* (discussed in the text) show that s.101(1)(c) is the gateway for previous relationship cases, but *R. v Haigh* [2010] EWCA Crim 90 tells us that it is also the gateway for background evidence cases (see at [23]–[25]), with the court there placing explicit reliance on the important dicta of Purchas L.J. in the common law case of *R. v Pettman* (to be found in the text at para.19–18).

fn.98 A similar type of warning about the danger of this gateway being made too wide was given in *R. v D, P and U* [2011] EWCA Crim 1474, where Hughes L.J. (V-P), having described it as "open to misuse", went on to say that it was designed to deal with, "the situation in which a jury cannot properly understand the case without hearing evidence . . . of bad character" (see at [22]).

fn.100 Another good example of a situation where no help was needed by the jury, in order for it to be able to understand the primary evidence, and where gateway (d) was the appropriate one to be invoked, is *R. v Saint* [2010] EWCA Crim 1924.

(f) *Important matters in issue between prosecution and accused*

The importance of the interaction between the three factors, relating to the strength   **19–24** of the bad character evidence itself, that were put forward in *R. v Hanson*, namely the number of convictions, the level of their similarity with the present alleged offence, and their age, is demonstrated by a number of recent cases. Though, as *Hanson* itself specifically mentions, similarities may properly be treated by the trial judge as making up for the fact that there is but one conviction, as in *R. v Tye* [2009] EWCA Crim 1738 and in *R. v Wehbe and Porter* [2011] EWCA Crim 978, it is implicit in the reasoning of Rose L.J. that they may also be capable of making up for the age of the one conviction. Thus, in *R. v Jasionis* [2010] EWCA Crim 2981, where the charge was one of rape, the judge had ruled that the accused's single conviction for a rape committed over twenty years before was admissible because of the strength of the similarities. The court upheld the judge, though, in doing so, it did point out that it would have been legitimate to overturn him only if his decision was one to which no reasonable judge could have come. In *R. v Turner and others* [2010] EWCA Crim 2300, the court was, on an application to it for leave to appeal, prepared to go further, and specifically to endorse the trial judge's decision, the main charge against Turner being murder, to allow evidence to be called of a conviction, some fifteen years before, of an offence of aggravated violence. Again, the basis for that decision was the strength of the similarities. In both *Jasionis* and *Turner and others*, the reasoning of the court in *R. v Murphy* (see the text at fn.106) was relied upon, so it is worth setting out here what Keene L.J. had to say, on this point (at [16]):

"There may be cases where the factual circumstances of just one conviction, even as long ago as 20 years earlier, *might* be relevant to showing propensity, but we would expect such cases to be rare and to be ones where the earlier conviction showed some very special and distinctive feature, such as a predilection on the part of the Defendant for a highly unusual form of sexual activity, or some arcane or highly specialised knowledge relevant to the present offence. In cases with less distinctive features in common, one would require some evidence of the propensity manifesting itself during the intervening period in order to render the earlier evidence admissible as evidence of a continuing propensity."

That passage was also quoted with approval in *R. v McGarvie* [2011] EWCA Crim 1414, but its application to the facts there led to the appeal being allowed. On charges of rape, attempted rape and sexual assault, the prosecution had been permitted to adduce evidence of similar convictions dating back, respectively, 33 and 18 years. The trial judge had allowed only the bare facts of conviction to be adduced, explaining that, where the defence was, as in the present case, consent, it was sufficient, for purposes of admissibility, that all the convictions were for sexual offences against a woman, without consent. Especially in view of the antiquity of the convictions, the appeal court considered that that level of probative value was quite insufficient to make it proper for them to be adduced.

A rather surprising example of similarity making up for age and singularity might seem to be *R. v Miller* [2010] EWCA Crim 1578. Miller faced five charges of rape of his niece, at dates when she would have been aged 11, and he 24 or 25, all of them being alleged to have taken place in the house where both lived. His defence being simple denial, the judge had permitted the prosecution to adduce evidence of Miller's conviction, some ten years before the present alleged offences, when he was only 16, of a "gang rape", in a car park, of a girl then aged 15 or 16. Faced with the obvious argument, on appeal, that the circumstances of the two cases were wholly different, the respondent argued that the common factor was an underlying abuse of power, in the earlier case the power of the numbers in the gang, in the later that flowing from the relationship and the difference in age. It was accepted by the court that that common factor was sufficient to justify the judge's conclusion that the evidence relating to the "gang rape" was capable of being evidence of propensity. That said, it is right to add that the defence had, for its own tactical reasons, invited the judge to rule only on the strict propensity point, without taking account of the potential for unfairness and prejudice to Miller arising from the age of the conviction or, indeed, from any other circumstances. Therefore, the appeal court was bound to apply a rather attenuated *Hanson* test, as regards the case for admission.

More surprising yet may be thought to be the decision in *R. v Jackson* [2011] EWCA Crim 1870. There, the charge being murder, the court upheld the trial judge's decision to admit a single conviction for that same offence, over twenty years before, simply on the basis that it established in the accused a propensity to carry out a serious attack by strangulation, which propensity was relevant (by reference to s.103(1)(a)— see para.19–29 below) to an important matter in issue, namely the identification of the killer, whose victim had also been strangled. The court referred to *R. v Murphy* (see above) without disapproval, so it seems that the key to the decision may have been that the court found itself unable to describe the decision of the trial judge as "plainly wrong" (see at [34]).

fn.106 One point to emerge from the alarming number of recent cases involving allegations of historic sexual abuse relates to the significance of the age of the conviction. Put simply, where the allegations concern events taking place, say, twenty years before, whatever be the force of the argument that paedophilic inclinations persist over long periods, if the conviction itself is of a similar age, then it goes towards establishing the relevant propensity at the time of the offences now alleged—see, e.g., *R. v Haystead* [2010] EWCA Crim 3221. Cf. the first note to para.18–20 above, where a similar point is made in the context of the law relating to good character directions.

fn.107 The defence argument that the prosecution is merely seeking to use the evidence of the accused's bad character to bolster a weak case continues to meet with little success. Thus, in each of *R. v James* [2009] EWCA Crim 2347, *R. v Kingdom* [2009] EWCA Crim 2935, *R. v Louis* [2010] EWCA Crim 735, *R. v Evans and Sabbagh-Parry* [2010] EWCA Crim 2253, *R. v Hedge and another* [2010] EWCA Crim 2252, *R. v Harding* [2010] EWCA Crim 2145, *R. v KW* [2010] EWCA Crim 2734 and *R. v Brown* [2011] EWCA Crim 80, that argument was rejected. Indeed, in a number of those cases, the appeal court expressed the view that the evidence apart from that of bad character was strong, not weak. In any event, these tend to be just the sort of cases where the court is likely to pray in aid the freedom of judgment of factual matters granted to the trial judge by the authorities, subject only to a finding of *Wednesbury* unreasonableness. That said, the argument did succeed in *R. v Bagot* [2010] EWCA Crim 1983, where the case for the prosecution was described as "comparatively thin" (see at [18]), though it has to be said that the bad character evidence there was of one offence, showing no great similarity to the offence charged, and committed some four years before, when Bagot was only fourteen, so that there was not much probative value therein to make up for the thinness of the rest of the case for the prosecution.

fn.109 The idea, emerging from the conjoined appeal of *Pickstone* in *R. v Hanson*, and applied in *R. v Cox*, that a sexual interest in young children is so unusual and persistent that even one, old example thereof will be capable of passing through gateway (d), was again applied in *R. v Haystead* [2010] EWCA Crim 3221. That the same notion applies to conduct that has not led to a conviction is demonstrated by *R. v Alec Edward A* [2009] EWCA Crim 513. There, the charges against the accused included one of rape, more than 25 years before, of his daughter, and the extraneous bad character evidence was contained in recent computer files that demonstrated his interest in father/daughter incest. The court was fully persuaded that this kind of sexual abnormality was as persistent as it was unusual. More recently, the court, in *R. v D, P and U* [2011] EWCA Crim 1474, has affirmed that a more general interest in child pornography is quite capable of demonstrating a sexual interest in children sufficient to be admissible on charges involving the (active) sexual abuse of them. That decision was later applied in *R. v Balcombe-Jestico* [2011] EWCA Crim 1630 to a case where, (i) the pornographic images had been created some 20 years *after* the alleged sexual assault, and, (ii) those images were of the broadest range of sexual activity, being, by no means, restricted to abuse of children.

fn.111 A more recent example, where the common law test would almost certainly   **19–25** have been satisfied, is *R. v Gumus* [2009] EWCA Crim 1355.

In the first subparagraph of para.19–25, in the text, the point is made that the emphasis, in the common law cases, was on previous criminality that had *not* resulted in conviction, whilst that, under the Act, has been firmly on convictions. That continues to be the case. Moreover, a point that has been taken, in some of the cases, is that, where there has been no conviction, particular care is required of the trial judge, because of the risk of the jury being distracted by the collateral issue that may well arise, as to whether or not the alleged other crime was actually committed—see e.g., *R. v Bill* [2010] EWCA Crim 612, at [19].

fn.112 In *R. v Rakib* [2011] EWCA Crim 870, the accused was alleged to have indecently exposed himself, on two separate occasions, to the same young woman. Her evidence was that, the first time, she had seen him masturbating his erect penis, but that, the second time, she had not looked towards his genitals. However, she had observed exactly the same motions of his left arm as on the earlier occasion, as she put it, "as if he were masturbating". The other circumstances in which these events took place were, she said, just as before. The court held that the evidence of the observed masturbating was admissible as circumstantial evidence that the accused had also been masturbating on the second occasion. Clearly, it was the (striking) similarity of the two events that led to this holding.

19–26   fn.117 The position taken in the text has found recent support in Redmayne [2011] Crim LR 177.

fn.118 The courts continue to find attractive the argument put by Moses L.J. in *R. v McAllister*. Three recent examples, in all of which the criminal conduct relied upon by the prosecution was extraneous to the case at hand, rather than charged as a separate count on the same indictment, are *R. v Ali* [2010] EWCA Crim 1619, *R. v Kamara* [2011] EWCA Crim 1146 and *R. v Cambridge* [2011] EWCA Crim 2009. In *Ali*, the court regarded the evidence in question as going to identity, rather than showing propensity (but see para.19–28 below). In *Cambridge*, where *Makin* was explicitly prayed in aid (at [9]), the evidence was regarded as admissible to rebut the accused's defence of innocent association.

In *Kamara*, the prosecution submitted that it was, "less a case of adducing bad character evidence to show propensity than one of advancing such evidence to prove knowledge or to rebut an innocent explanation" (at[18]). It seems that Richards L.J. could see the fallacy in the argument, since, though he accepted that submission, he entered the following qualifying words (at [21]):

> "... the previous convictions ... were plainly relevant to the issue of lack of knowl-edge or innocent association, and in this case too the different ways of expressing the matter—whether by reference to propensity, coincidence or innocent association—can be seen to be to some extent interrelated, albeit that the true focus is ... on the rebuttal of the defence of innocent association."

The facts of the case neatly demonstrate why it is so important to appreciate that it was indeed propensity that was being relied upon by the prosecution. Large quanti-ties of drugs, as well as drug paraphernalia and large sums in cash, had been found at premises where Kamara's co-accused resided, but at which he spent time, as well as keeping there some of his possessions. Indeed, some of the drugs had been found in a rucksack that belonged to him. His defence to the joint charges of possessing drugs with intent to supply was that he knew nothing of the drugs or money, which must have belonged to his co-accused. It must have seemed clear to Richards L.J. that the argument for admitting evidence of a conviction, less than three years before, of a similar offence, though expressed in the terms it was by counsel, depended upon propensity reasoning: it was the propensity that the conviction demonstrated that rebutted innocent association, coincidence, or whatever one wants to call it. Nothing has changed since the then L.H. Hoffmann argued, in 1975, that the key to avoiding error with regard to similar fact evidence was that one must not erect "a distinction between different *kinds* of relevance when the true distinction is between different *degrees* of relevance" (see (1975) 91 L.Q.R. 193, at 200 (emphasis in original). And, even in *Kamara*, where the commonsense argument for admission seems so strong, it may be that, if one articulates that one really is relying on propensity, there is less danger of one underestimating the possibility that the co-accused was an equally active drug dealer who might have had good reason for seeking to put the blame on

Kamara, and who might even have planted drugs in the rucksack, as Kamara was, by implication, alleging.

fn.121 In *R. v Sandom* [2010] EWCA Crim 2124, objection was (surprisingly) taken, on appeal, to the fact that, in what counsel suggested was a non-propensity case, with evidence of Sandom's bad character going to rebut coincidence, the trial judge had given the jury a propensity direction. Dismissing that objection, the court observed that this was, "one of those cases where the jury might find the evidence on one count both such as to negative coincidence and to establish propensity" (at [15], per HH Judge Gilbert, QC). Perhaps one might be forgiven for suggesting that that remark rather gives the game away.

It is noted in the text that *R. v Freeman and Crawford* entails the reasoning in *R.* **19–27** *v McAllister* applying no less to cases involving arguments for cross-admissibility of evidence relating to counts on the same indictment than to evidence of criminality extraneous to the matters at hand. In both *R. v Norris* [2009] EWCA Crim 2697 and *R. v Bryan Andrew B* [2010] EWCA Crim 1257, the court explicitly applied that reasoning to a cross-admissibility case.

It is pointed out in the text that a preference for the "pooling approach" over the "sequential approach" was expressed in *R. v McAllister*, for identity cases, and in *R. v Freeman and Crawford*, for cases where the defence was that no offences had been committed. However, in *R. v Norris* [2009] EWCA Crim 2697, the defence was, in effect, a mixture of the two. Five elderly patients, being treated in orthopaedic wards at two hospitals at which Norris had been working as a nurse, had all fallen into hypoglycaemic comas, yet none of them was diabetic. Four had died, while one, having recovered, had died several months later from an unrelated cause. Norris was charged with four counts of murder and one of attempted murder, the prosecution case being that the comas had been brought about by his improper injection of the victims with insulin. His twofold defence was that, if injections of insulin had indeed been the cause of the comas, then there was another nurse that could have done the injecting, but that, in any event, it was not as improbable as the medical experts were saying that the excess of insulin in the blood might have arisen naturally. The trial judge most certainly directed the jury to adopt a sequential approach, telling them first to consider one of the counts, on its own, in order to decide whether or not Norris had injected that person with insulin, and only if they concluded that he had, then to go on to consider what effect that conclusion properly had upon their consideration of the other counts (see at [57]). The court explicitly endorsed the judge's approach (see at [80]), so the case clearly tells against the "pooling approach" that was favoured in both *McAllister* and *Freeman and Crawford*. It seems to follow that the issue of which approach ought to be followed remains unsettled.

As has been pointed out in the note to fn.118, in para.19–26 above, *R. v Ali* [2010] **19–28** EWCA Crim 1619 was treated by the court as a case not involving the bad character evidence being relied upon for propensity purposes, but as supporting a disputed identification of the accused. However, the evidence at issue, on charges of murder and of attempted murder involving use of firearms, was contained in photographs of the accused holding firearms and two sets of body armour, and in the statement of a witness who claimed that he had seen Ali stroking his beard with a gun. In truth, the evidence did show a propensity in Ali to be involved with firearms, so that the better case for its admission, rather like that in *R. v Purcell*, was that, though not exhibiting any features of similarity with the matters charged, it had high probative value, *as propensity evidence*, in supporting the identification in question. Equally, in *R. v Harding* [2010] EWCA Crim 2145 (see, also, *R. v Onya* [2010] EWCA Crim 2985), Harding, accused of robbery at a dwelling-house, sought to explain the presence of his DNA on a glass at the scene as having resulted from being given a drink by his co-accused, whilst both were innocently present there. The court upheld the judge's decision to permit the prosecution to rebut that explanation by reference to his nine previous convictions for robbery, even though similarities with the present charge were not relied upon.

Nor should it be forgotten that there are cases where the prosecution really does not rely on propensity at all. For example, in *R. v Hamidi and another* [2010] EWCA Crim 66, part of the defence to a charge of conspiracy to cheat the Revenue was that any part played by Hamidi had been as an innocent agent. He had been interviewed about involvement in a similar fraudulent conspiracy, several years before, but not subsequently prosecuted. However, the prosecution argued that, because, during the course of that interview, Hamidi had got to know how his involvement, innocent or otherwise, had facilitated the fraud, it followed that it was less likely that he would have been innocently involved in the fraud on the present occasion. The court upheld the trial judge's ruling that that evidence was admissible. Though the prosecution was not, for that reason, relying upon Hamidi's propensity, it must be said that it is then not entirely easy to see how the evidence revealed his bad character either.

(i) *Matter in issue*

19–30   fn.152 In *R. v Rycroft* [2010] EWCA Crim 2705, the court seemed to support the trial judge's line of reasoning, which had been similar to that taken in *R. v Belogun*, though no reference was made to that case, whilst *Rycroft* itself involved only an application for leave.

(ii) *Relevant to an important matter*

19–31   fn.158 The quoted statement from *R. v Tully and Wood* was applied in *R. v Thomas and others* [2010] EWCA Crim 148.

The significance of the need to identify, with precision, to which issue of importance the evidence is said to be relevant, as emphasised in both *R. v Bullen* and *R. v McCarry and Waters*, has continued to loom large in the cases. A good example of a case where, like in *Bullen*, the evidence was found not to be relevant is *R. v Feeley* [2010] EWCA Crim 1836. There, a tube of jelly, designed for sexual lubrication purposes, had been found in the accused's bathroom cabinet. The charges against him included counts of anal rape. The court overturned the trial judge's decision to allow evidence of the finding of the tube to be adduced. As Aikens L.J. succinctly put it (at [36]):

> "[i]t does not even prove that the appellant was in the habit of using [the] jelly to lubricate his penis for the purpose of any type of intercourse, let alone for the purposes of anal rape in a period of over 1 year before the jelly was found".

The opposite result was reached in *R. v Harris* [2011] EWCA Crim 912, though, it is submitted, equally persuasively. There, the defence to a charge of possession of cocaine with intent to supply was that, though he used cocaine, he dealt only in cannabis. Given that defence, it is hardly surprising that the court was satisfied that his conviction for possession of cocaine with intent to supply was relevant to an important matter in issue between the parties. Likewise, in *R. v Mockble* [2010] EWCA Crim 2540, the prosecution case, on a charge of murder, was that Mockble had, having left the scene of an earlier confrontation, turned his car around and deliberately driven it back, at speed, such that it collided with the victim. Mockble's explanation for the turnaround being that, having realised that his passenger had been injured in the earlier confrontation, he was driving back to seek first aid, the prosecution was permitted to adduce evidence of his convictions for offences of violence, all of which had resulted from angry public confrontations. Mockble's application for leave to appeal was rejected, on the basis that those convictions tended to rebut his explanation. One must remember that the issue here is one of technical legal relevance, so that, even where the strength of the evidence might seem to be rather slight, it may well suffice, especially when one recalls the considerable margin of appreciation allowed to the trial judge. Instructive examples are to be found in *R. v Maina* [2010] EWCA Crim 3228, *R. v Olu and others* [2010] EWCA Crim 2975; [2011] 1 Cr.App.R. 404, *R. v Okenarhe* [2011] EWCA Crim 616 and *R. v Nicholas and Dennie* [2011] EWCA Crim 1175.

A fresh point arose in *R. v Slack and Johnson* [2010] EWCA Crim 1149. On a murder charge, the case against Johnson had initially been that she had herself, whilst drunk, engaged in the violent attack that had resulted in the death of the victim in his flat. The prosecution was permitted to adduce evidence of her convictions for violent attacks upon people in their own homes, after she had been drinking. The trial then took a turn such that the prosecution was now alleging, not that Johnson was herself was one of the assailants, but that she had encouraged those that had carried out the fatal attack. The court upheld the trial ruling that the evidence in question remained properly before the jury, since it was "artificial to suggest that a propensity to drunken violence cannot be relevant when considering drunken encouragement to violence" (see at [26], per Maurice Kay L.J.). See *R v Cambridge* [2011] EWCA Crim 2011 as an example of the principle that the gateway is not limited to cases of 'propensity'.

(iii) *Special rules for convictions*

Though *R. v Atkinson* was not referred to in *R. v Morgan* [2009] EWCA Crim 2705, the court there assumed that an offence of the same description does not necessarily demonstrate a propensity to commit offences of the kind charged, since it was only the fact that previous sexual offences, like the present ones, involved the accused seeking sexual gratification by attacking vulnerable children when in a position of trust, that persuaded it of the existence of a specific enough propensity.   **19–32**

fn.177 In *R. v O* [2009] EWCA Crim 2919, though *R. v Hassan* was not cited, a similar willingness to allow latitude to the prosecution was demonstrated. In a classic similar fact case, had the victim of the earlier sexual offences been called to give evidence herself, it would have been for a third time, since the jury had disagreed at a first trial. The court thought that the trial judge had been right, rather than putting her through that, to allow the details to be brought out through the particulars of the offences, as stated in the indictment.   **19–33**

(iv) *Fairness of the proceedings*

Another case in which the view was taken that s.101(3) involves a discretion to exclude, not a rule of exclusion is *R. v Bill* [2010] EWCA Crim 612.   **19–35**

19–37   *R. v DS* [2010] EWCA Crim 1016 neatly illustrates the special kinds of prejudice that may result from there having been a considerable lapse of time between the earlier matters demonstrating bad character and the present charge(s). There, an allegation of a sexual offence, by the accused against his niece C, dated back to 1972. Some of the factual detail related to the part played by C's grandmother in the aftermath of the alleged events, but the grandmother was dead. Moreover, C alleged that the offence had taken place in the accused's house in Scotland, yet he denied having had such a house before 1975. In that respect, no Council records now existed of when he had taken on the tenancy. Because of the potential for prejudice to the accused flowing from those matters, the court overturned the trial judge's decision to allow the evidence to be adduced.

Of course, in assessing the case for ruling out evidence of old matters, the court will have firmly in mind the probative force of that evidence, on the particular facts—see *R. v Withers* [2010] EWCA Crim 3238, and R v Jackson [2011] EWCA Crim 1870.

(g) *Proof and prejudice*

(i) *Probative value*

19–43   fn.215 The proposition in the text is too baldly stated. As was pointed out in *R. v N(H)* [2011] EWCA Crim 730 (at [40], per Pitchford L.J.):

> "[c]ontamination (deliberate or innocent), if it has or may have occurred, may render unreliable the evidence of one or more Complainants whether or not the jury is invited to consider whether their evidence is mutually supportive. Where such a real possibility is revealed by the evidence we accept that there will be an obligation upon the trial judge to draw the jury's attention to the risk."

It is to be noted that *R. v King* was specifically relied upon by the court.

19–44   fn.220 Further confirmation of the fact that the 2003 Act leaves the decision in *R. v Z* untouched is contained in *R. v Hamidi and another* [2010] EWCA Crim 66 (at [34]), where *Z* was cited, and by *R. v Wiltshire* [2010] EWCA Crim 1874, where it was not.

fn.222 That the 100 per cent credibility rule *does* apply to acquittals is confirmed by *R. v Morgans* [2010] EWCA Crim 3089 (at [23]).

Morgans also deals with a point raised in the text following fn.222. The verdict in question there had been a formal one of not guilty, entered by the trial judge when the prosecution offered no evidence, and without the accused being put in the jury's charge. Thus, the principle stated in *R. v Z* certainly embraces that kind of case. Some might find it a little strange that evidence that the prosecution was not even prepared to put before a jury at one trial was deemed 100 per cent credible, for admissibility purposes, at another.

In *R. v Small* [2010] EWCA Crim 3241, Small had been acquitted by the jury, but on the direction of the judge, of being knowingly concerned in the importation of prohibited drugs, on the basis that there was insufficient evidence of a nexus between Small, the importation and the courier to establish *knowing concern*. His defence to two fresh but similar charges was that, though there was evidence linking him both with the couriers and with the importations, those links were matters of innocent coincidence. The court upheld the trial judge's decision to admit evidence of the facts behind the earlier acquittal, saying (at [21]):

"It was not the fact of his acquittal which was probative. Rather what was probative was the evidence—which was not in dispute and was set out in the admissions—that the applicant had on a previous occasion gone to the airport to meet a courier who had imported cocaine from the same country and in the self-same fashion, namely by secreting the drug in foodstuffs (bread rolls), as the two importations with which the applicant was alleged on this indictment to have been knowingly concerned."

In short, there was no challenge to the acquittal. Rather the facts establishing his physical involvement with the earlier importation were such as to make it unlikely that, on the later occasions, he would have been equally lacking in knowledge as he may have been on the earlier one. In fact, the probative use of the evidence was rather similar to that suggested by Lord Hobhouse of Woodborough in *R. v Z* itself as being possible, without challenging the acquittal itself (see [2000] 2 A.C. 483, at p.509C, and see, also the explanation of *R. v Ollis* [1900] 2 Q.B. 758 offered by Salmon L.J. in *G v Coltart* [1967] 1 Q.B. 432, at p.440). Just the same sort of reasoning was relied upon by the respondent, and apparently endorsed by the court, in *R. v Hamidi and another* [2010] EWCA Crim 66.

fnn.223 and 224. A third situation, where, though there had been no acquittal,   **19–45**
proceedings had terminated favourably to an accused, is shown by *R. v Hamidi and another* (cited in the preceding note). As in *R. Nguyen*, no criminal proceedings had been brought against Hamidi, but, in addition, a VAT tribunal had made a ruling that must have entailed it taking him to have had no fraudulent intent on the earlier occasion, when one of the matters denied by him in the later proceedings was presence of that intent.

fn.226 Concerns about the dangers of diversion and deflection of the jury's reasoning by satellite issues have continued to be of particular moment for the court where there has been some official ruling or decision tending to the innocence of the accused, in relation to the earlier matters relied upon that demonstrate the accused's bad character—see, e.g., *R. v Wiltshire* [201] EWCA Crim 1874 (at [10]) and *R. v Morgans* [2010] EWCA Crim 3089 (at [28])

There have been several recent cases in which the appellant has sought to rely upon   **19–47**
dissimilarities as denying sufficient probative force to the evidence of extraneous bad character. Little would be gained by detailed discussion of them here. Where, as is almost inevitably the case, there are both similarities and dissimilarities, a great deal turns upon the significance attached by the court to the individual elements. Two cases in which greater significance was found in the similarities are *R. v Thomas and others* [2010] EWCA Crim 148 and *R. v Wehbe and Porter* [2011] EWCA Crim 978, whilst two in which it was found in the dissimilarities, are *R. v Clements* [2009] EWCA Crim 2726 and *R. v Bagot* [2010] EWCA Crim 1983, in both of which cases the appeal was, in consequence, allowed. Still, the number of similarities, combined with the paucity of dissimilarities, may also be a factor in the trial judge's decision being affirmed. For example, in *R. v BLW and RAH* [2010] EWCA Crim 1738 (see, also, *R. v Arshad* [2011] EWCA Crim 2048), the sole dissimilarity relied upon was that the female complainants in the sexual offences charged were prepubescent, while the one in the extraneous matter was a pubescent. The court was much more persuaded by the similarities that all had taken place in a familial context, that the accused had befriended a parent or parents of the relevant complainant, before committing the

alleged offences, and that all had been committed in breach of trust. To be contrasted with that case is *R. v McKenzie* [2011] EWCA Crim 1550, where the obvious dissimilarity was that, while the complainant in the present case was a young male, the one in the extraneous case, was a young female, but the more significant one that the former concerned active sexual interference, the latter a mere suggestion that she have sex with him.

Though it is rather obvious, it does bear pointing out that similarities (or, for that matter, dissimilarities) may legitimately be prayed in aid only where they are demonstrated by some evidence in the case—see *R. v Fyle* [2011] EWCA Crim 1213.

(ii) *Prejudicial effect*

19–51   In both *R. v A* [2009] EWCA Crim 513 and *R. v Unwin* [2011] EWCA Crim 23, the trial judge had been pressed, in effect, with an argument in terms of the "bad person" prejudice, but had rejected it. The basis for that argument, in both cases, was that, if it was revealed to the jury that the accused in question had, on his computer, thousands of "lurid and revolting" images of children engaged in acts of vaginal and anal penetration, etc., they would be unable fairly to try the present charges of rape and indecent assault of children. In *A*, the appeal court upheld the judge, though without addressing specifically that particular element of prejudice, while, in *Unwin*, the court granted an application for leave, on the basis that the judge had not given reasons for his ruling, both in relation to this point, and in relation to others raised by the applicant. It remains to be seen what the court will make of the argument when it hears the appeal proper. It should be added that, in neither case, had the jury been shown the images, as opposed to having been given a description of them, something later described, by the court in *R. v D, P and U* [2011] EWCA Crim 1474, at [11], as "a sensible practice which should generally be adopted".

A slightly different form of the "diversion prejudice" was relied upon in *R. v Fyle* [2011] EWCA Crim 1213 as one reason for allowing the appeal. The court considered that, because the accused had challenged the extraneous evidence, there was a very real danger of prejudice, in that, if the jury were not persuaded that his testimony on that matter might be true, they might take the credibility of his testimony directly in relation to the offence charged as highly damaged.

19–52   fn.241 Two later cases in which the point made in the attached text has been stressed are *R. v DS* [2010] EWCA Crim 1016 and *R. v Rhodes* [2010] EWCA Crim 2771. As we have seen, this same point, often described as involving the need to avoid satellite litigation or issues, has also arisen in cases where there has been some official ruling or decision tending to the innocence of the accused (see note to fn.226 above).

(h) *Non-criminal acts or facts and surrounding circumstances*

19–54   fn.251 The courts have not yet definitively addressed the question of how use of evidence of extravagant lifestyle, and, in particular, possession of large amounts of cash, in drugs cases, is to be treated under the 2003 Act. Though it is hard to see how this can fail to amount to evidence of bad character (unless some argument under s.98(a), that it has to do with the facts of the offence charged may, on the particular facts, be relied upon), what authority there is tends to treat it as not comprehended by the Act at all—see *R. v Graham* [2007] EWCA Crim 1499 and *R. v Green, Wilson and Austin* [2009] EWCA Crim 1688.

An instructive example of a case where apparently innocent behaviour took on its   **19–55** dark side from the context is *R. v Rossi* [2009] EWCA Crim 2406. The allegations against Rossi were that he had watched two boys urinating in a public lavatory in St. Paul's Cathedral, then masturbated in front of one of them. His defence being that, though he had been there, he had not done anything as alleged, the prosecution was permitted to adduce evidence that he was often seen sitting outside the lavatory in question, and that he would go into it only after young boys had themselves gone in. An argument that mere presence outside a lavatory in a public space could not be reprehensible was rejected by the court, which pointed out that the effect of the prosecution evidence was that he was not waiting outside it for innocent reasons.

The cases concerned with what constitutes "reprehensible behaviour" still do not   **19–56** reveal a consistent and coherent understanding of that term, with reprehensibility seeming to be a matter in the eye of the individual judicial beholder. That said, one can understand why, in *R. v Scott* [2009] EWCA Crim 2457, a s.100 case, the court distinguished false allegations from a complainant that a potential witness for the defence had sexually assaulted her, as well as placing faeces on her doorstep, both of which allegations counted as reprehensible behaviour by her, from more generalised allegations that the complainant had harassed a friend of the accused with regard to the charges against him, which did not. In *R. v Saint* [2010] EWCA Crim 1924, it was alleged that the accused, then a park ranger, had a habit of patrolling the park at night, wearing both face paint as camouflage and night vision goggles, in order secretly to observe couples engaged in sexual intercourse in parked vehicles, as well as that he had an interest in "swinging parties". The court was satisfied that both the habit and the interest were reprehensible (though it went on to rule that the evidence in question should not have been admitted, since both of slight probative value and considerable prejudicial effect). More surprising, perhaps, is *R. v Delaney* [2010] EWCA Crim 105. There, the court did not reject counsel for the appellant's argument that photographs of one Tabrett, who alleged that he had been unlawfully wounded by Delaney, showing him stripped to the waist and in a boxer's stance, must be tested for admissibility under s.100. (Delaney's defence was self-defence.) One may also be surprised by *R. v Yusuf* [2010] EWCA Crim 359, another s.100 case. There, a rape complainant had set in motion a substantial police investigation, identifying three suspects, but had then failed to co-operate with the police in a number of ways, such that police resources were wasted. The court had no doubt that this conduct was reprehensible. Though her conduct was certainly very unsatisfactory, one does wonder, especially in view of the nature of the complaint, if it should really be accounted reprehensible.

A new point arose in *R. v Ali* [2010] EWCA Crim 1619. Photographs of Ali holding body armour and firearms (apparently not real ones) had been taken in Pakistan. Equally, a statement of a witness that he had seen Ali stroking his beard with a gun, it must be assumed, also concerned events in Pakistan. In that country, the handling of guns is not criminal. Therefore, held the court, neither the photographs nor the statement disclosed an offence or reprehensible behaviour. The offence aspect seems clear enough, though the decision as to reprehensibility might seem to leave open a rather worrying argument that that issue should be judged by social standards specific to a given section of the population of a country.

(i) *Directions to the jury*

19–57   The failure of the trial judge to direct the jury that they must not, simply because of the previous convictions, treat the accused as either untruthful as to the present matters, or guilty of the present charge, were treated in *R. v Ellis* [2010] EWCA Crim 163 as important omissions, though the court went on to hold that the conviction had not, thereby, been rendered unsafe.

    fn.269 Lord Phillips C.J's advice that the direction must not be made to follow a rigid formula, but must be tailored to the specific facts of the case was followed in *R. v Ferdhaus* [2010] EWCA Crim 220 (at [10]), whilst his comment that failure to give a direction that would have amounted to no more than assistance to the jury in applying common sense would not amount to error is supported by *R. v Marsh* [2009] EWCA Crim 2696 (at [57]).

19–58   fn.273 Though no reference was made to *R. v McDonald* in *R. v Bill* [2010] EWCA Crim 612, the effect of the latter case is exactly the same as the former. Indeed, the appeal was allowed purely because the jury had been told that evidence that had been admitted for its relevance to the issue might be used by them as relevant to the accused's credibility.

(l) *Rules of Court*

19–61   fn.292. Another case affirming that that is the correct approach is *R. v Ramirez* [2009] EWCA Crim 1721.

BAD CHARACTER OF THE ACCUSED (DEFENCE ASPECTS)

2.—CRIMINAL JUSTICE ACT 2003

(c) *Evidence given for the accused*

R. v Garnham was followed in *R. v Gruber* [2010] EWCA Crim 1821. In *R. v Tollady* **20–06**
[2010] EWCA Crim 2614, the court referred to both *R. v Highton* and *R. v Campbell*,
though not to *Garnham* or *Gruber*. Though it seemed to recognise that *Highton* suggests that, once evidence has been adduced by the accused, *mere* relevance should
suffice to allow it to be used by the prosecution, as going to the accused's credibility,
it went on to say that the evidence in the case at hand was not *sufficiently* material to
credibility to be so used.

(d) *Correcting a false impression*

(ii) *Loss of "shield"—assertion elements*

fnn.37 and 38 A salutary warning was given, in *R. v D, P and U* [2011] EWCA Crim **20–14**
1474, of the danger of judicial over-reliance upon s.101(1)(f). Hughes L.J. (V-P) reiterated that a mere denial cannot constitute the giving of a false impression, going on to
point out that any such impression must, in any event, have been given by the accused
to the court (see at [21]).

fn.43 In *R. v Tod* [2011] EWCA Crim 463, the accused, when asked in evidence—it
is not clear whether in-chief or in cross-examination—why he had chosen to make no
comment in response to questions put to him by the police, had replied that he had,
while acting as a solicitor's representative for twenty years, always advised clients
not to comment, so was acting upon that advice himself. The trial judge treated that
evidence as creating the impression of the accused's respectability within the legal
system, and as *intended by him* so to do. Therefore, the judge ruled that a conviction
for an offence of bribery as a serving police officer was admissible against him, to demonstrate the falsity of the impression. The court regarded the reasons for that ruling
as entirely sound. Though one may question the notion that, given the way in which
the evidence from the accused came out, he should have been taken to have intended
to make the respectability claim, the case does support the suggestion in the text that
an intention to assert is required.

(iii) *Loss of "shield"—false impressions*

20–17   In *R. v Chrysostomou* [2010] EWCA Crim 1403, the accused, charged with an offence of possession of firearms and one of harassment, had, for his own tactical reasons, admitted, in his evidence, to being a drug user, though not to being a dealer. The court ruled that the trial judge had been wrong then to allow to be adduced, prosecution evidence, contained in text messages in the accused's mobile telephone, suggesting that he was, in fact, a drug dealer. It reasoned that, there being no other material suggesting the falsity of the impression in question, it had been wrong to allow it to be shown by "the very evidence that the Crown wished to adduce, viz the texts" (see at [37], per Aikens L.J.) Though it is true that the police had come by this material adventitiously, when searching for evidence from the telephone that might have, more directly, addressed the charges at hand, it did indeed suggest that the accused was a dealer, so would appear to have had probative value, in credibility terms, in correcting the impression originally given.

(e) *Attacks on another person's character*

(ii) *The protected class*

20–25   That it is important to be clear about the precise effect of the limitation to the protected class stated by Keene L.J. in *R. v Nelson*, and quoted in the text, is demonstrated by *R. v Wild* [2011] EWCA Crim 358. Jumaa, the person whose character had been attacked (through evidence of his convictions for offences of violence) had not testified, but it was the prosecution case that he had very probably been the person that Wild and others had attacked, as part of the events that led to the charges of affray against them. Wild's defence was that he had been defending himself against Jumaa's attacks. Though it quoted Keene L.J's words, the court ruled that the trial judge had been right to allow Wild to be cross-examined about his own convictions for dishonesty and drugs offences. The result seems entirely consistent with the spirit of *Nelson*, in that, though Jumaa was not, in a technical sense, a "victim" (since an affray cannot have an individual victim), he was, most certainly, as it is put in the text, a person playing a part in the drama.

(iii) *The meaning of "attack"*

20–31   It is now abundantly clear that the moderation of the application of s.101(1)(g) in favour of the accused, recognised by *R. v Britzman* under the 1898 Act, is indeed comprehended by s.101(3). Three recent cases support that position, which was, previously, most plainly taken in *R. v Lamaletie and Royce*, but not, on the better view, denied in *R. v Singh*. The three cases are *R. v O* [2009] EWCA Crim 2235, *R. v Chisholm* [2010] EWCA Crim 258 and *R. v Woodhead* [2011] EWCA Crim 472. In *O*, it was argued for the appellant that the defence to charges involving violence, which was that he had been defending himself, amounted only to an emphatic denial (more properly, a necessary attack). The argument was rejected, but only because the defence actually involved the further imputation that the complainants had colluded in telling lies to the court. Such a basis for allowing cross-examination about convictions is entirely consistent both with the common law and with the earlier cases under the 2003 Act (see the text to which fnn. 103 to 107 are attached). The defence's reason for invoking s.101(3), for these purposes, in *Chisholm* was that it had been the prosecution that had initially put forward the bad character of three of its witnesses, with the defence merely adding to that "attack". The reason for this strange turn of events was that the three of them were alleged to have been involved in an attack, involving a gun, upon Chisholm's son, a few months before. The prosecution case was that the present charge arose from a revenge attack by Chisholm and others, including his son. For his part, Chisholm sought to explain why, on this occasion, he had been carrying a knife, his son an axe. He said that it was for protective purposes, arising not only from the attack on the son, but also from other violent and threatening things that the three witnesses had said and done. Presumably, it was cross-examination about those things that had been added to the prosecution's initial "attack". Though the appeal court clearly took the point about the prosecution having initially brought out the bad character of its witnesses, it regarded itself as not in as good a position as the trial judge to evaluate the full extent of the additional defence attack, since it had not been invited to read the transcripts of the defence cross-examination.

Finally, in *Woodhead*, it was the *scale* of the attack on the complainant that persuaded the appeal court that the trial judge had been right not to disallow evidence being given of the accused's convictions, under s.101(3). Though it rejected the argument that it should take into account, and apply, the cases under the pre-Act law, it added the following important comment (at [23], per Thomas L.J.):

> "In this particular case it is said that we ought to have regard to the old law for the purpose of looking at the way in which the questioning took place and the extent of the allegations made in deciding whether the evidence of bad character should be admitted. However, it seems to us that that is a matter that a court would take into account under the law as set out in s.101(3) in appropriate cases."

This is as clear an indication as one could have that it is no less right for the courts to prevent from arising the broader type of tactical unfairness to the accused than it was before the 2003 Act became law. Though the courts' desire not to be swamped by pre-Act cases is entirely understandable, it might help them to formulate some principles of application, under the new law, were they to be referred to *Britzman* and *R. v St.Louis and Case* (see fn.100 in the text), under the old.

(iv) *The permissible evidential purpose*

Though most of the cases continue to be consistent with the wide view of credibility taken, for example, in *R. v Singh* and *R. v Bahanda*, *R. v Chrysostomou* [2010] EWCA Crim 1403 strikes a very different note. In that case, part of the defence case, on charges of possession of a firearm with intent to cause fear of violence and of harassment, was that he had gone to see the complainant (in relation to both offences), in order to get her to repay £750 that she owed him. His counsel had been permitted to cross-examine her about alleged drug use, the context therefore seemingly being that his conduct, including the admitted breaking of a window at her house, had been insistent because of fear that the cost of her drug habit would make her unable or unwilling to repay her debt. The court overturned the trial judge's decision to allow evidence of his own apparent dealing in drugs to be adduced under s.101(1)(g), on the basis that it had no relevance to the charges against him, "other than to blacken [his] general character in the eyes of the jury and, therefore, dent the credibility of his evidence generally" (see at [40], per Aikens L.J.). The court appears not to have had the benefit of citation of any of the relevant authorities. In consequence, it is unsurprising that, when counsel for the appellant in the later case of *R. v Clarke* [2011] EWCA Crim 939, relied upon

20–33

Chrysostomou, the court, though without explicitly saying that that case was wrongly decided, reiterated that the law was as stated in *Singh*, *Bahanda* and a number of other post-Act authorities. In particular, it was not at all an argument for excluding such evidence that it would tend aversely to affect the accused's general credibility.

fnn.133 and 134 *R. v O* [2009] EWCA Crim 2235 and *R. v Woodhead* [2011] EWCA Crim 472 are two more cases confirming that it does not matter that the bad character evidence goes, more obviously, to the issue of guilt than to credibility. Indeed, in *O*, the court gave, as its reason for upholding the trial judge, that, where the defence to two charges of wounding was self-defence, the jury were entitled to know, in assessing whether the complainant or the accused was more likely to have reached for a bladed article, that the latter had, only a few months before, been convicted of possession of a Stanley knife. So, though neither *R. v Letts and Chung* nor *R. v Wilson* (see fn.135) was referred to, similar reasoning was clearly applied. In R v Williams [2011] EWCA Crim (no transcript yet) the Court of Appeal overturned the finding of the trial judge admitting the evidence of W's three previous convictions on the ground that there was a clear risk that the jury would have treated the convictions as evidence of propensity, as opposed to just W's credibility. The judge had also not directed the jury in clear terms as to the limited purpose – credibility of such evidence.

(v) *Proof and prejudice*

20–37   It is clear from *R. v Chrysostomou* [2010] EWCA Crim 1403 that it is entirely proper to take account of moral prejudice to the accused when considering whether to disallow, under s.101(3), evidence that satisfies s.101(1)(g).

(vi) *Judicial directions*

20–38   *In R. v Q* [2011] EWCA Crim 1824, where the charge was one of assault occasioning actual bodily harm the accused's previous convictions were for police assaults, minor public order offences and offences of dishonesty. He having alleged that the assault had been carried out by a prosecution witness and a third party, the judge had allowed those convictions to be adduced in evidence to help the jury to decide "what the truth is". Though no cases were relied upon by the court, in upholding a direction to the jury, to that effect, its decision that the direction was legally sound seems entirely consistent with the statement of Hooper L.J. in *R. v Lafayette*. Where various evidence is admitted under multiple gateways, a careful direction should be given as to what evidence is being admitted under which gateway, and for what purpose: *R v DF* [2011] EWCA Crim 2168. See also *R v SW* [2011] EWCA Crim 2463, the Court of Appeal held that the trial judge had given insufficient guidance to the jury on the critical question of cross-admissibility – there was a danger that despite the brief direction to give separate consideration to each court, the jury was bring invited to form and overall view. See *R v H* [2011] EWCA Crim 2344, where the Court, reviewing the relevant authorities, the court considered in detail the question of the cross-admissibility of complaints, and the need for a direction on the independence of the evidence.

(g) *Spent convictions*

20–43   In *R. v Jasionis* [2010] EWCA Crim 2981, the court rejected a submission on behalf of the appellant that it was relevant to whether or not the prosecution should be able to adduce evidence of his Lithuanian conviction (for rape) that the conviction was "spent", according to the law of that country. What seems not to have been noticed by the court is that the provisions of the 1974 Act, and, presumably, therefore, those of the Consolidated Criminal Practice Direction, apply to convictions outside Great Britain (see s.1(4)(a)) (It may be that, because of the length of any sentence of imprisonment that may have been imposed by the Lithuanian court, the conviction was one that would never become spent, under English law, in any event.)

CHAPTER 21

BAD CHARACTER OF THE CO-ACCUSED

2.—CRIMINAL JUSTICE ACT 2003

(a) *Introduction*

fn.1 As long as the defence of the accused has not been conducted in the way that **21–02** was envisaged in *R. v Jones, Devall and Gordon*, a matter will not be put in issue by evidence adduced in the case that, though admissible for some purpose, is inadmissible as against the co-accused. This interesting ruling was made in *R. v Miah and Choudhury* [2011] EWCA Crim 945. There, Choudhury did not testify, but relied in his defence to a charge of murder, in part, upon his statement to the police. That was in the nature of a mixed statement, having inculpatory elements, but also exculpatory ones, so must have been admitted in evidence for the truth of both elements by virtue of *R. v Sharp* [1988] 1 W.L.R. 7 (on which, see the text at paras 36–34 and 36–35). However, it also contained material firmly implicating Miah in the murder. Had that material been admissible against Miah, there would undoubtedly have been an important matter in issue between the two of them, in relation to which Choudhury's conviction for robbery might well have been regarded as having substantial probative value. The court ruled that, because it was inadmissible hearsay, as regards Miah, no such matter was properly in issue between them. Presumably, counsel for Choudhury had conducted the case in a way that did not thereby entail the issue being joined with Miah under *Jones, Devall and Gordon*.

(b) *The general test*

R. v Loftus and Comben [2009] EWCA Crim 2688 would seem to pose difficulties, **21–04** having regard to the wording of s.101(1)(e), rather like those that might arise were the facts similar to those of *R. v Miller* to crop up under the 2003 Act. Loftus's defence to a charge of historic sexual abuse (some thirty years before) of his then partner Comben's two children, aged eight and six, was simple denial. Comben, charged with the wilful neglect of those children, arising from her alleged failure to do anything to prevent the actions constituting that abuse though present when they had taken place, seems to have answered that either they had not taken place at all, or that, if they had, she would have been so frightened of Loftus that she would have felt compelled not to intercede. The trial judge allowed her to adduce evidence that Loftus had obliged her to engage in anal intercourse and other sexual practices to which she objected, as support for her contention that she was in his thrall. The court had no doubt that that evidence was admissible for her under s.101(1)(e). The difficulty here is that it was no part of Loftus's case that Comben was not in his thrall. Rather, the issue between the two of them was whether or not the abuse had actually taken place, yet the allegations about sexual practices had no relevance thereto.

21–05   fn.10 Of course, if there is nothing demonstrated by the bad character evidence that is capable of bearing any probative value for the co-accused as regards the issue in question, it will necessarily fail the test of substantial probative value, whether that test imports nothing beyond "real" or "not minute", or imports something more—see *R. v Malik* [2011] EWCA Crim 1306.

(e) *Absence of leave requirement*

21–16   *R. v Musone* was cited with approval in *R. v Ramirez* [2009] EWCA Crim 1721, though the court found, on the facts of that case, that there had been no manipulation of the rules. In *R. v Mitchell* [2010] EWCA Crim 783, the trial judge had ruled that the co-accused might adduce evidence of a very specific aspect of Mitchell's bad character, namely his tendency to give strikingly similar innocent explanations of his possession of dangerous implements. This was in order to allow support to be provided, via the unlikelihood of the same explanation being true on each occasion, for the co-accused's case that it had been Mitchell, not he, that had had possession of a firearm with intent to endanger life, which was the offence charged against both of them. However, counsel for the co-accused had then cross-examined Mitchell, more generally, to the effect that he had a propensity, as shown by the extraneous matters, to carry dangerous weapons. The court held that the cross-examination had been illegitimate because it had gone beyond the scope and purpose of the ruling. It is worthy of note that the court pointed out that no "application" had been made to the judge, to adduce this further evidence. Whether one refers to the giving of leave, or to permission being granted, or whatever, the effect would seem to be much the same.

CHAPTER 22

BAD CHARACTER OF PERSONS OTHER THAN THE ACCUSED

2.—THE COMMON LAW

(b) *Credibility relevance*

(i) *Party's own witness*

Another good example of a party revealing the bad character of its witness, because **22–11** evidence thereof has relevance to the issue, like *R. v Ross*, is *R. v Chisholm* [2010] EWCA Crim 258. There, the prosecution was allowed to show that the accused had a motive for violence against the complainants, flowing from the latter's own violent activities, and, in particular, a serious attack, involving a firearm, upon the accused's son (who was a co-accused).

3.—CRIMINAL JUSTICE ACT 2003

(a) *The basic provision and its scope*

In *R v Reid* [2011] EWCA Crim 2162, the Court of Appeal stated that, referring to **22–19** *R v Apabhai* [2011] EWCA Crim 917, that the word 'substantial' in s.100(1)(b) means that the evidence concerned has something more than trivial probative value.

fn.57 The recent authorities on s.98(a) and (b) of the act are considered in the notes to para.19–21 above.

fn 64 Although in *R v J (DC)* [2010] EWCA Crim 385; [2010] 2 Cr. App. R. 2 the **22–20** Court ordered disclosure of documents from social security files to undermine the credibility of some of the witnesses for the prosecution. Subsequently, the parties agreed pursuant to s100(1)(c) that all the documents could be put before the jury. The Court of Appeal held that where there was an order for disclosure in respect of matters in social security files relating to a person who was not a defendant, that order was limited and did not entitle either party, for example, to put the documents before the jury on the basis that its contents were admissible under the hearsay provisions of the Criminal Justice Act 2003—to do so would require a separate application to the judge who would consider the public interest immunity position. The requirement for such an order could not be circumvented by agreement between the advocates pursuant to s100(1)(c).

(b) *Important explanatory evidence*

22–21   A good example of a "background evidence" case under s.100(1)(a) is *R. v NK* [2009] EWCA Crim 2425. There, the jury had been denied information about convictions of, and sentences of imprisonment served by, the complainant of sexual offences alleged to have taken place over twenty years before the trial. One reason that the court had for allowing the accused's appeal was that evidence thereof was needed to render comprehensible the timetable of events, as related by the complainant, the accused and another witness, all of whom had impliedly used those convictions and sentences as reference points in their narrative of events, yet without being able to reveal them explicitly.

(c) *Substantially probative evidence*

(i) *Issue relevance*

22–23   fn.79 A good post-Act example of a case involving evidence that was relevant to the issue, but not via reasoning from propensity, is *R. v NK* [2009] EWCA Crim 2425, where the delay of twenty years in a complaint being made of sexual abuse was rendered harder to understand by the complainant's repeated contacts with the police, probation officers and other persons in authority, whilst being himself subjected to the rigours of the criminal justice system.

22–24   fn.84 Firm support for the position taken in *R. v S* is provided by *R. v GH* [2009] EWCA Crim 2899; (2010) 174 J.P. 203, where, having described the concept of "reverse propensity" reasoning as curious (at [17]), the court went on to apply such reasoning (albeit without referring to *S* itself).

22–25   It continues to be a matter of doubt precisely what the word "substantial", qualifying "probative value", entails. In *R. v Scott* [2009] EWCA Crim 2457, itself a case concerned with relevance to credibility, and not to the issue, Aikens L.J. said (at [45]) that the word:

> "must mean that the evidence concerned has something more than trivial probative value but it is not necessarily of conclusive probative value."

It will be appreciated that there is a considerable gap between non-triviality and conclusiveness, so the observation is rather tantalising, though it is entirely consistent with the idea that non-trivial (or real, or non-minute) relevance does suffice. By contrast, in the important reported case of *R. v Braithwaite* [2010] EWCA Crim 1082; [2010] 2 Cr.App.R. 18, whilst stressing the fact dependence of the judgment of the degree of probative value here, Hughes L.J. (V-P) did say that, in some quarters, it had been suggested that it imported a test of "enhanced probative value"—perhaps the "quarters" which he had in mind were, or included, para.363 of the Explanatory Notes to the 2003 Act (see the text at fn.87). Though he then refused to endorse that suggested gloss on the statutory wording, he did say that there was a distinction between the test and that of simple relevance (see at [15]). It will be appreciated that simple (legal) relevance may properly be accounted the same as non-trivial, non-minute or real relevance.

The text fails to refer to the fact that s.109 of the 2003 Act applies no less to evidence of the bad character of a non-accused than to that of the bad character of an accused. In *R. v Baxter* [2011] EWCA Crim 1767, the court did point out that, because of s.109, there is a need, in assessing the probative value of a witness's evidence, to assume its truth, for the purposes of s.100. The evidence there was that a rape complainant had, previously, admitted to the witness that she had falsely alleged that she had been raped, on another occasion, by the witness's son.

Of course, where the matter in issue in relation to which the evidence of another's bad character is said to have substantial probative value is not itself raised by other *evidence* in the case, that bad character evidence will have no probative value, whether substantial or otherwise. For example, in *R. v Badza* [2009] EWCA Crim 2695, the accused, charged with murder, sought to adduce evidence of material, including a conviction, suggesting that the deceased was a racist, in support of his position that the deceased had subjected him to racial abuse immediately prior to the incident resulting in his death. However, the accused had not given evidence, and witnesses, asked by his counsel about the alleged racial abuse, had denied that they had heard any. Hence, "[t]here was . . . no witness evidence of racial abuse" (see at [53], per Sir Anthony May P.). A case to similar effect is *R. v Mount* [2010] EWCA Crim 2974.

(ii) *Credibility relevance*

The question of what kinds of misconduct are to be regarded as relevant to cred-   **22–28**
ibility has continued to be given conflicting answers in the cases. In what may turn out to be a leading case, because officially reported, namely that of *R. v Brewster and Cromwell* [2010] EWCA Crim 1194; [2011] 1 W.L.R. 601; [2010] 2 Cr. App.R. 149, support was explicitly given to the view of credibility relevance taken in *R. v Stephenson*, with the view taken in *R. v S* being, equally explicitly, rejected. The court (at [22], per Pitchford L.J.) added the following gloss that may, or may not, be found helpful by its addressees:

> ". . . the trial judge's task will be to evaluate the evidence of bad character which it is proposed to admit for the purpose of deciding whether it is reasonably capable of assisting a fair minded jury to reach a view whether the witness's evidence is, or is not, worthy of belief."

The way in which the court went on to apply the law to the facts does rather suggest that it was, in fact, the view taken in *R. v Renda (Osbourne)* that it favoured. Though the bulk of the convictions about which the trial judge had refused the defence leave to cross-examine the complainant were for offences of dishonesty, one was for manslaughter. In ruling that cross-examination as to them all should have been allowed, the court pointed out that the facts relating to the manslaughter conviction had relevance to an issue in the case, but then added that it, no less than the other convictions, was "relevant in the wider sense as going to a fair minded jury's proper assessment of the standing of the witness" (at [24]). The earlier case of *R. v NK* [2009] EWCA Crim 2425 seems to be to similar effect.

To be set against those cases are *R. v Ul-Haq* [2010] EWCA Crim 1683 and *R. v South* [2011] EWCA Crim 754. In the former, the trial judge had clearly taken an approach to the convictions of a key prosecution witness the same as that required by *R. v Hanson*, for cases under s.101(1)(d). On appeal, counsel relied on *R. v Stephenson*, but the court upheld the judge, even though the convictions were principally for offences of dishonesty. The court did not have the advantage of being referred to *Brewster and Cromwell*, which had been decided only a month before. The court in *South* was referred to *Brewster and Cromwell*, though it seems not to the key paragraphs in the judgment. The trial judge had allowed a defence witness to be cross-examined about some 53 convictions, all for offences of dishonesty, but only 12 of which involved some element of deception. The court ruled that he had been right as to the 12, but wrong as to the remaining 41. Though mention was made of no other case, this case, just like that of *S*, plainly involves the application of the *Hanson* reasoning to s.100(1)(b).

It is submitted that this issue is one in need of authoritative clarification. It might be thought reasonable to add that the cases in the Court of Appeal are in such disarray that a trip to the Supreme Court is urgently required.

That non-accused are now placed in a distinctly more favourable position than accused, as regards arguments about their credibility, is, in two respects, strikingly shown by the cases of *R. v Myers* [2010] EWCA Crim 3173 and *R. v Townson* [2011] EWCA Crim 63. In the former, on a charge of aggravated burglary, the prosecution had, under s.101(1)(d), been permitted to adduce evidence of his two convictions for that same offence. The defence then sought leave to cross-examine the complainant about his convictions for sexual offences and offences of violence, on what was candidly accepted as being a "tit for tat" basis. The court upheld the trial judge's refusal of leave. In doing so, it specifically rejected the argument that the attack on the accused's character made any difference to the admissibility calculation under s.100(1)(b). Of course, had it been the accused that had taken the first step, in attacking the character of the complainant, the prosecution would have been at liberty to pray in aid s.101(1)(g), as regards the accused's convictions, even had they been ruled inadmissible under s.101(1)(d).

In *Townson*, the charge being manslaughter, the defence self-defence, counsel for the accused sought leave to have admitted, under s.100(1)(b), evidence of the bad character of the deceased, and, in particular, evidence that in 2005, about three years before his death, when 15–years-old, he had been, (i) ejected from the Territorial Army for aggressive and argumentative behaviour that could result in violence, (ii) referred to the Community Mental Health Team for aggressive and impulsive behaviour, and (iii) reported to the police, by his mother, for threatening, whilst holding a kitchen knife, to go to kill a named individual. Leave having been refused, the prosecution had then adduced evidence of the deceased's "laid-back attitude" and friendliness. Unsurprisingly, and no doubt with the analogy to s.101(1)(f) in mind, the defence renewed its application, in relation to the 2005 events, but it was again refused. The court upheld the judge, commenting that those events had taken place a considerable time before the death, as well as that, by then, the leopard seemed to have changed his spots. Even without reference to the evidence that the prosecution had adduced, this reasoning might not be such as to convince everyone that the 2005 events did not have substantial probative value on the issue of self-defence. Given that they had heard evidence of the deceased's friendly, laid-back attitude, without correction of what would surely have been treated as a false impression, had the issue arisen under s.101(1)(f), the jury would surely have found it rather hard to believe he could possibly have been the aggressor, especially when the defence had, no doubt to forestall the prosecution, put in evidence the accused's convictions for violence. Though it may be that the absence of any language in s.100(1)(b) equivalent to that in s.101(1)(f) and (g) may properly have the effects revealed by *Myers* and *Townson*, the result of those two cases is most assuredly that sauce for the goose is not sauce for the gander.

The reported cases of *R. v Braithwaite* [2010] EWCA Crim 1082; [2010] 2 Cr.App.R.   **22–31**
18 and *R. v Miller* [2010] EWCA Crim 1153; [2010] 2 Cr.App.R. 19 bring some clarity to the issue of when, if ever, mere allegations of criminal conduct may be adduced in relation to a witness. First, where the opposing party is in a position only to invite admissions thereof from the witness in cross-examination, there will be very little likelihood of leave being granted, since there would, in those circumstances, be no evidence of wrongdoing before the court, with the result that a speculative foray into the witness's character, of a kind that s.100 was (in part) designed to prevent, would have been allowed. Furthermore, as *Braithwaite* expressly decides, a mere allegation in a CRIS (Crime Reports Information System) police report is most unlikely to clear the hurdle of substantial probative value, since it would merely record that the allegation had been made, and this would be especially the case if the allegation had later been withdrawn (as in *R. v Bovell and Dowds*). On the other hand, as Hughes L.J. (V-P) put it, in *Braithwaite* (at [20]), "[i]t might be different if hard evidence of the allegation were to become available and if that is what the Applicant were to seek to adduce". With respect, the latter point must be correct, notwithstanding a suggestion in *Bovell and Dowds* to the contrary. Where there is *evidence* of the matter at hand, s.109 is no less applicable to s.100 cases than to s.101 ones, and it states that the relevance or probative value of evidence is to be assessed "on the assumption that it is true". This must apply equally to allegations against a witness as to those against an accused. In fact, that ought to apply no less to allegations in CRIS reports, as long as admissible despite their hearsay nature, albeit subject, no doubt, in the case of those later withdrawn, to the s.109(2) power in the court not to assume truth where no court or jury could reasonably find the allegation to be true.

fn.118 Further cases on the meaning of "reprehensible behaviour" are dealt with in   **22–32**
the notes to para.19–56 above.
An allegation that a complainant of a sexual offence has previously falsely claimed some third party to have committed a sexual offence against her will clearly amount to an allegation of "reprehensible behaviour", so, as in *R. v Baxter* [2011] EWCA Crim 1767, may well need to be considered under s.100, as well as under s.41 of the Youth Justice and Criminal Evidence Act 1999 (as to which, see below at para.22–39).

fn.131 A further case on the police misconduct issue discussed in the text is *R. v*   **22–33**
Francis [2011] EWCA Crim 375.

4.—Special Protection From Bad Character Evidence (Rape and Allied Offences)

22–35   Further, helpful discussion of the relationship between the s.100 and s.41 tests is to be found in *R. v Scott* [2009] EWCA Crim 2457 (see at [57]-[63]). That discussion is entirely consistent with the holding in *R. v V*, to which case reference was made.

(b) *The position under statute*

22–38   fn.154 That a key to the proper application of the fairness test announced in *R. v A (No.2)* is a careful assessment of the full facts of the case was emphasised in *R. v S* [2010] EWCA Crim 1579. The accused, charged with the rape of his wife, wished to adduce evidence of an occasion, about a week before the events at issue, when the two of them had had consensual sexual intercourse. The court affirmed the judge's ruling against the accused, on the basis that other evidence in the case, in fact from the complainant herself, established that there had been a sexually active relationship between them in the weeks before the alleged rape, albeit one that caused her unhappiness.

fn.158 *R. v Uddin and others* [2010] EWCA Crim 1818 provides further support for the proposition that reading down may be required in third party cases.

(i) *Scope of the Act*

22–39   In *R. v Uddin and others* [2010] EWCA Crim 1818, the court clearly assumed that evidence that the complainant was pregnant was evidence of "sexual behaviour", though one wonders whether it was really about a result thereof, rather than about the behaviour itself.

Something of a tension has emerged in the most recent cases as to precisely how strong is the test of "proper evidential basis" for an allegation of a previous false complaint. In *RD* [2009] EWCA Crim 2137, though without making reference to *R. v AM* (now known as *R. v Murray*), Keene L.J., the author of the judgment in *R. v T, H*, stated that it required a "much more solid foundation" than that provided by cross-examination about inconsistencies in what the present complainant had said in relation to her earlier complaint (see at [18]). In *R. v Scott* [2009] EWCA Crim 2457 (see also, *R. v Davifar* [2009] EWCA Crim 2294), the court, having had the advantage of being referred to *T, H*, to *Murray* and to *RD*, chose to read *RD* as not derogating from the principle stated in *Murray*, though it must be added that, on the facts of that case itself, the defence did have, in its hands, evidence of falsity, so was not dependent upon cross-examination of the complainant herself to establish an inference thereof. Most recently, in *R. v E* [2009] EWCA Crim 2668, the court doubted that there was a significant distinction between *Murray*, on the one hand, and *T, H* (and, by implication, *RD*), on the other. In doing so, it did refer to "material" capable of supporting the inference of falsity, which could clearly be found in statements of the complainant, no less than those of others, and it does not seem that the defence had available, in that case, any (admissible) evidence to show falsity, before seeking to embark on cross-examination of the complainant. Despite these recent judicial claims of consistency, it does seem that there is a real disagreement, in need of resolution, between the position taken in *Murray* and that taken in *RD*.

In *R. v Baxter* [2011] EWCA Crim 1767, the court made it clear that, as long as there is a proper evidential basis for the defence claim that a false allegation had previously been made by the present complainant, it does not matter that the latter denies making any allegation at all, rather than admitting making the allegation, but denying its falsity.

fn.165 In R v E [2011] EWCA Crim 2393, the Court of Appeal upheld the finding of the trial judge that the complainant's previous fake allegation of rape did not fall within s.41, because it was not questioning about her sexual behaviour, but her actions in telling lies.

fn.172 There is now explicit authority, under the 1999 Act, that "sexual behaviour" can be carried out by one person alone—see *R. v Ben-Rejab and Baccar* [2011] EWCA Crim 1136. There, the court first stated that viewing pornography, or engaging in sexually-charged messaging over a live internet connection, were "plainly" embraced by the term. It then went on to hold that answering sexually explicit questions in quizzes, because that activity too must be designed for the obtaining of sexual pleasure, was equally comprehended by it.   **22–41**

(ii) *The grounds for leave*

fn.193 That the hurdle erected by *R. v A (No.2)* is a significant one is confirmed by both *R. v Uddin and others* [2010] EWCA Crim 1818 (as to which, see the note at para.22–38, fn.158 above) and *R. v MM* [2011] EWCA Crim 1291 (as to which, see the following note to fn.195).   **22–46**

fn.195 The court in *R. v MM* [2011] EWCA Crim 1291 emphasised that evidence of *particular* instances of previous consensual sexual relations between the complainant and the accused failed to demonstrate any adequate, relevant similarity with the presently alleged conduct that constituted the offence of rape. In this respect, the mere "parallels" that existed between them, in terms of the nature of the intercourse, and where it had taken place, were of insufficient significance, especially having regard to the fact that the jury was, via a formal admission, already aware of the *general* nature of relevant elements of that previous sexual relationship.

fn.208 Another example of evidence regarded as relevant to support the credibility of the accused's own account of events would appear to be *R. v Harling* [2010] EWCA Crim 2949.   **22–47**

The suggestion in the text, flowing from *R. v Rooney*, that a claim made by the complainant of *non*-behaviour must count as "sexual behaviour" may be cast into doubt by *R. v Krasniqi* [2011] EWCA Crim 2026. There, charged with rape, the accused had admitted to having lain on the bed next to the complainant, but had denied having had sexual intercourse with her. Her testimony had included a claim that she would not have intercourse with anyone whilst menstruating (as she admittedly was, at the time). The defence sought leave to rebut that claim under s. 41(5), by adducing evidence that traces of the semen of a third party had been found on the knickers that she had been wearing at the time. The court ruled that the trial judge had been right to refuse leave. It reasoned, first, that the evidence could not be brought within "the limited terms of s. 41(5)" (see at [9]), and, secondly, that, in any event, it failed to satisfy the additional test set by s.41(2)(b) (as to which, see the note below to para.22–50). Since it seems clear that the evidence did not go further than necessary to   **22–48** rebut her claim (under s.41(5)(b)), the implication is that her evidence was not "about [her] sexual behaviour" (under s.41(5)(a)). However, the court failed explicitly to say that a claim not to have intercourse when menstruating does not constitute sexual behaviour, and its emphasis was on the s.41(2)(b) point, describing it as presenting the accused with an "insuperable obstacle" (at [9]). It must be said that, were such a narrow view of "sexual behaviour" to prevail as a matter of ordinary interpretation, it is hard to believe that the special canon under s.3(1) of the Human Rights Act 1998 (on which see *R. v Hamadi* , in the text) would not convincingly be prayed in aid to ensure fairness to the accused.

22–49   It was envisaged in *R. v Uddin and others* [2010] EWCA Crim 1818 that s.41(6) might, in a suitable case, have to be read down, under the fairness principle announced in *R. v A (No.2)*, in order to allow a complainant to be asked if she was a prostitute, though the facts of the case itself did not, in the judgment of the court, give rise to such a need.

22–50   In *R. v Krasniqi* [2011] EWCA Crim 2026 (the facts of which are related at para.22–48 above), the court took a view of s.41(2)(b) that *does* suggest that the unsafe conviction test laid down there is akin to that applicable, generally, to appeals (under s.2(1)(a) of the Criminal Appeal Act 1968. The court ruled that evidence of the finding of traces of the semen of a third party on the complainant's knickers was inadmissible because of s.41(2)(b), explaining that the defence, "faced the insuperable obstacle that the presence of the semen could not be said to be probative of sexual intercourse, as opposed to any other form of sexual activity" (see at [9], per Holroyde J.). This does suggest that the subsection sets a very high hurdle, since, in circumstances similar to those in *Krasniqi* itself, evidence of the finding of an accused's semen on the complainant's underwear, as evidence of the fact of intercourse, must be commonly adduced.

CHAPTER 23

LEGAL PROFESSIONAL PRIVILEGE

1.—THE NATURE OF LEGAL PROFESSIONAL PRIVILEGE

(j) *Who is a lawyer for the purpose of claiming privilege*

If the client in good faith instructs someone whom he believes to be a lawyer he can **23–24** claim privilege even if unbeknown to him the person he instructed was not a lawyer because he had been struck off: *Dadourian Group International Inc v Simms 2008* EWHC 1784 (Ch) Patten J.

In *Prudential Assurance v Special Commissioners of income Tax* [2010] EWCA Civ 1094 the Court of appeal reaffirmed the principle that communications with tax accountants cannot attract legal advice privilege. The Supreme Court has subsequently given permission to appeal.

(k) *EU law and in-house lawyers*

Akzo Nobel was affirmed by the ECJ on September 14, 2010. **23–26**

3.—PARTS OF DOCUMENTS, SELECTIONS AND COPIES

(d) *The Lyell v Kennedy exception*

See *Imerman v Tchenguiz 2009* EWHC 2902 (QB) Eady J **23–49**

4.—PARTICULAR CASES

(f) *Conditional fee agreements*

23–56 An after-the-event insurance policy was not privileged: *Barr v Biffa Waste Services* [2009] EWHC 1033 TCC Coulson J. The contrary view was taken by the QB Senior Master in *Pedro Emiro Florez Arroyo v BP Exploration Co (Columbia)* 6.5.2010, unreported.

6.—LEGAL ADVICE PRIVILEGE

(e) *The* Balabel *test after* Three Rivers

23–88 In *C v C 2007 WTLR 753* Munby J the argument that a solicitor's conveyancing file was not covered by legal advice privilege was unsurprisingly rejected.

7.—LITIGATION PRIVILEGE

(c) *Whose purpose?*

23–91 See *Westminster International BV v Dornoch* [2009] EWCA Civ 1323.

(e) *Litigation in reasonable prospect*

23–95 Christopher Clarke J considered in *Axa Seguros SA De CV v Allianz Insurance Plc* [2011] EWHC 268 (Comm) the dividing line between circumstances which afford a reasonable prospect of litigation on the one hand (which were subject to litigation privilege even if litigation could not be said to be more probable than not) and a mere possibility of litigation on the other hand. The fact that one or more conditions have to be fulfilled in order for a dispute to arise which requires the commencement of litigation in order to resolve it did not necessarily mean that litigation was only a possibility.

23–97 See *Westminster International BV v Dornoch* [2009] EWCA Civ 1323.

OTHER FORMS OF PRIVILEGE

1.—JOINT PRIVILEDGE

In *Ford v FSA* [2011] EWHC 2583 (Admin) the Court considered for the first time,   **24–01**
the extent to which a former CEO could enjoy joint privilege with the company (now
in administration) in communications from lawyers who were formally only retained
by the company. In finding that the claimant did enjoy joint privilege, the court set out
five criteria to be applied, namely:

(1)   that he communicated with the lawyer for the purpose of seeking advice in an
       individual capacity;
(2)   that he made clear to the lawyer that he was seeking legal advice in an indi-
       vidual capacity;
(3)   those with whom the joint privilege was claimed, grew or ought to have appre-
       ciated the legal position;
(4)   the lawyer knew or ought to have appreciated that he was communicating with
       the individual in an individual capacity and
(5)   that the communication with the lawyer was confidential (see para.40 of the
       judgement).

3.—WITHOUT PREJUDICE PRIVILEGE

(c) *When is correspondance treated as within the without prejudice rule?*

Whilst it is not conclusive whether or not the letter is marked without prejudice,   **24–21**
it is highly relevant: see *Williams v Hull* [2009] EWHC 2844 (Ch) Arnold J at [41]
and *Prudential Assurance v The Prudential Assurance Co* [2002] EWHC 2809 (Ch)
at [18].

An apparently open letter which contained threats was not to be treated as without
prejudice because its concluding paragraphs contained an offer; it was more in the
nature of a letter before action: *Best Buy Co Inv v Worldwide Sales Corp Espana* [2011]
EWCA Civ 618.

(e) When without prejudice correspondence may be admitted in evidence

24–24   In *Oceanbulk Shipping and Trading v TMT Asia Ltd* [2010] UKSC 44 the Supreme Court held that without prejudice material was potentially admissible as part of the factual matrix for the purposes of construing a contract concluded after without prejudice discussions.

(f) The three-party situation

24–27   In *Williams v Hull* [2009] EWHC 2844 (Ch) Arnold J said at [23] that it was not correct to dissect a communication into parts, to determine whether all the parts are without prejudice unless it is concerned with distinctly different subjects.

In *R v K* [2009] EWCA Crim 1640, [2010] QB 343, the Court of Appeal considered whether a third party into whose hands evidence of damaging admissions made in the course of without prejudice communications had fallen was entitled to rely on those admissions in subsequent proceedings against the party who made them. The Court held that the public interest in prosecuting crime was sufficient to outweigh the public interest in the settlement of disputes and therefore that admissions made in the course of "without prejudice" negotiations were not inadmissible simply by virtue of the circumstances in which they were made.

(j) Admissibility of without prejudice negotiations in interim applications

24–35   In *Linsen International ltd v Humpuss Sea Transport* [2010] EWHC 303 Christopher Clarke J considered the authorities on need for disclosure of without prejudice materials in making an ex parte application. The judge pointed out that in general it was not open to one party unilaterally to disclose without prejudice materials and that such disclosure might in the event unfairly prejudice the other party. Thus usually it would not be for the party seeking the order to make such disclosure. However, the obligation of the party seeking the order was to ensure that the court was not misled and a party might give himself problems by sweeping statements as to the evasiveness of the other side where disclosure of without prejudice negotiations might give a different impression. It might be appropriate to make some disclosure without making disclosure of the detailed content.

(m) Unambiguous impropriety

24–41   It is insufficient to make out a case of unambiguous impropriety that a party is putting forward a contention at odds with his pleaded case: *Williams v Hull* [2009] EWHC 2844 (Ch) Arnold J at [58]. The judge referred to Rix LJ in *Savings & Investment Bank v Fincken* [2004] 1WLR 667 at [57] when he said that it was not an abuse of the without prejudice privilege to tell the truth even if it is inconsistent with your pleaded case. That paragraph of *Fincken* was approved by Lord Brown in *Bradford & Bingley v Rashid* 2006 1WLR 2066 at [65].

24–45   See *Woodward v Santander UK plc*, EAT [2010] IRLR 834.

4.—PRIVILEGE AGAINST SELF-INCRIMINATION

(g) *How great must the risk be?*

See *Phillips v Newsgroup* [2010] EWHC 2952 Ch.   **24–72**

(n) *Statutory abrogation: construing the statute*

In *Gray v News Group Newspapers* [2011] EWHC 349 (Ch) Vos J held that privilege   **24–90** against self-incrimination could not be claimed where it was alleged that the defendants had intercepted messages to the claimants' voicemail boxes. The withdrawal of the privilege in s72 of the Senior Courts Act 1981 covered proceedings for infringement of rights pertaining to any intellectual property, and "intellectual property" was defined to include "technical or commercial information", and meant any such information which could be protected as such by action. See also *Phillips v Newsgroup Newspapers* [2010] EWHC 2952 (Ch) Mann J.

The Matrimonial Causes Act 1973 s25 together with r2.61 of the Family proceedings Rules abrogated the privilege in ancillary relief proceedings. Information so obtained was thus under compulsion and would be inadmissible in other proceedings: *R v K* [2009] EWCA Crim 1640.

The Fraud Act 2006 s13 had removed the privilege against self-incrimination in relation to s328 of the Proceeds of Crime Act 2002: *JSC BTA Bank v Ablyazov* [2009] EWCA Civ 1124.

CHAPTER 25

FACTS EXCLUDED BY PUBLIC POLICY

2.—PUBLIC INTEREST IMMUNITY TODAY

(e) *Government procedure*

See in relation to the December 1996 paper *R (Mohamed) v Secretary of State for*   **25–14**
Foreign and Commonwealth Affairs [2008] EWHC 2010.

3.—PUBLIC INTEREST IMMUNITY IN PRACTICE: CRIMINAL CASES

(c) *Inadvertent disclosure*

On loss of public interest immunity by inadvertent disclosure see *R (on the appli-*   **25–22**
cation of Pewter) v Commissioner of Police for the Metropolis, QBD (Wilkie J)
3.12.2010, unreported.

4.—PUBLIC INTEREST IMMUNITY IN PRACTICE: CIVIL CASES

(b) *Public interest immunity in civil cases today*

It is not open to the court to order a closed material procedure in an ordinary civil   **25–25**
claim for damages: *Al Rawi v Security Service* [2010] 3 WLR 1069.

The importance of the accuracy of the ministerial certificate was stressed by Laws   **25–26**
LJ in *R (Al Sweady) v Secretary of State for Defence* [2009] EWHC 1687 (Admin).

CHAPTER 26

LOSS AND WAIVER OF PRIVILEGE

1.—WAIVER OF PRIVILEGE: THE PRINCIPLES

(b) *Loss of confidentiality different from waiver of privilege*

In *Osland v Secretary to the Department of Justice* [2008] HCA 37 the attorney-general set up a panel of QCs to advise him whether a petition of mercy should be granted to a person convicted of murder. The petition was rejected and the attorney-general issued a press release which stated "the joint advice recommends on every ground that the petition should be denied." The question whether there was a waiver of privilege was rejected by the High Court of Australia, upholding the decision of both lower courts. There was no inconsistency between disclosing the fact of, and the conclusions of, the independent advice and wishing to maintain the confidentiality in the advice itself. This was not the case of a party to litigation deploying a partial disclosure for forensic advantage while seeking unfairly to deny the other party an opportunity to see the full text of the privileged communication. Nor was it the laying open of the confidential communication to necessary scrutiny.

26–03

2.—EXPRESS WAIVER OF PRIVILEGE

(e) *Waiver of privilege in criminal cases*

The authorities referred to in this paragraph were considered in *R v Seaton* [2010] EWCA Crim 1980 when *R v Wilmot* was explained.

26–17

3.—LIMITED WAIVER

(b) *Effect of waiver in first proceedings on use by same party in subsequent proceedings*

26–22   See *Balu v Dudley Primary Care Trust* [2010] EWHC 1208 (Admin). In *Re Scottish Lion Insurance Co Ltd* [2011] CSIH 18 the Scottish Inner House distinguished cases such as *Dennis Rye* and held that creditors of an insurance company who had disclosed privileged documents for the purposes of having their claims valued for the purpose on voting of a scheme of arrangement could not claim privilege for the documents in proceedings for the sanctioning of the scheme because a claim for privilege in those proceedings would be inconsistent with their prior disclosure. However, the court would protect the confidentiality of the documents as it did not discount the possibility of a claim for privilege in relation to them in a different context.

4.—WAIVER OF PRIVILEGE: WAIVER EXTENDING TO COLLATERAL OR ASSOCIATED DOCUMENTS

(b) *"Deploying in court"*

26–27   See *Halahan v Spain* [2011] EWHC 621 Admin, Wilkie J.

(c) *Deployment in interlocutory proceedings and at trial*

26–31   In *Berezowsky v Abramovich* [2011] EWHC 1143 (Comm) the Claimant had for the purposes of a summary judgment hearing waived privilege over interviews between solicitors for the Claimant and a witness who had subsequently died. After the summary judgment application had been dismissed, the Defendant sought disclosure for the purposes of the trial of collateral or associated material recording or reflecting the content of interviews by the claimants' lawyers with the witness on the ground that there had been a waiver of privilege. The claimant argued that the summary judgment application had been disposed of, that no decision had been taken whether to waive privilege at trial, and that in those circumstances fairness did not require disclosure of associated material. Gloster J ordered disclosure. She held that where privileged material was relied upon for the purpose of an interlocutory hearing, fairness did require disclosure of associated material even though the application was made after the application had been disposed of. The single possible exception to the rule was where the issue in the interlocutory application was not an issue at the trial.

(d) *"The issue in question"*

26–34   See *Dore v Leicestershire CC* [2010] EWHC 34 (Ch) Mann J. In *Digicel (St Lucia) Ltd v Cable & Wireless plc* [2009] EWHC 1437 (Ch) Morgan J pointed out at [31] that as waiver is judged objectively, the fact that a statement is made that a reference is not to be taken as a waiver does not prevent the court holding that as a matter of law the statement does constitute a waiver. See in care proceedings *Re D (a child)* [2011] EWCA Civ 684.

6.—IMPLIED WAIVER OF PRIVILEGE

(a) *The principle of implied waiver*

Morgan J expressly followed *Farm Assist v Secretary of State for Environment Food and Rural Affairs* [2008] EWHC 3079 (TCC) in *Digicel (St Lucia) Ltd v Cable & Wireless plc* [2009] EWHC 1437 (Ch). It had been argued that the putting in issue of the state of mind of certain individuals could not fairly have been decided by the court without reference to legal advice they had received (a submission which was contrary to the Court of Appeal decision in *Paragon v Freshfields* [1999] 1 WLR 1183*)*. See also *Mac Hotels Ltd v Rider Levett Bucknall UK* [2010] EWHC 767 (TCC). **26–59**

8.—LOSS OF PRIVILEGE THROUGH FRAUD

(b) *To what sort of fraud does the rule apply?*

See *Owners of the Kamal XXIV v Owners of the ship Ariela* [2010] EWHC 2531 (Comm) Burton J. **26–72**

CHAPTER 27

THE COLLATERAL UNDERTAKING

	PARA.
1. Development of the undertaking	27–02
2. The position under the CPR	27–09
3. Arbitrations	27–20
4. Obtaining permission to use the documents	27–22 ∎
5. Termination of the undertaking	27–27

4.—OBTAINING PERMISSION TO USE THE DOCUMENTS

(a) *Principles on which leave is given*

Permission to disclose documents to the revenue was refused as unnecessary and **27–23**
unjustified in *Sita UK Group Holdings Ltd v Serruys* [2008] EWHC 869, although the
applicant should not be prevented from answering questions raised by the revenue
and could use knowledge obtained from the documents for that purpose

THE RULE AGAINST HEARSAY

2.—Definitions of Hearsay

In *Horncastle v R* [2009] UKSC 14 at [20) Lord Phillips said that at common law   **28–03**
hearsay evidence was:

"any statement of fact other than one made, of his own knowledge, by a witness in
the course of oral testimony."

He added that hearsay evidence:

"was inadmissible even if it was a past statement made by someone who was called
to give oral evidence and who could be cross-examined about it. Furthermore,
hearsay evidence was inadmissible, whether it assisted the prosecution or the
defence."

3.—Justifications For the Hearsay Rule

In *Horncastle v R* [2009] UKSC 14 at [21] Lord Phillips said that there: **28–08**

"were two principal reasons for excluding hearsay evidence. The first was that it
was potentially unreliable. It might even be fabricated by the witness giving evidence of what he alleged he had been told by another. Quite apart from this, the
weight to be given to such evidence was less easy to appraise than that of evidence
delivered by a witness face to face with the defendant and subject to testing by
cross-examination."

At [27] suggested that that the "best evidence" rule only justified the hearsay rule in
relation to a witness who was available to give evidence.

4.—Application of the Hearsay Rule at Common Law

(c) *Res gestae and original evidence*

28–25   fn.147 Evidence of conduct admitted as original evidence under the res gestae doctrine extends to the conduct of the victim of the offence. Res gestae permits the adduction of evidence of incidents connected to the charge. In *O'Leary v The King*, this Court held that, on a charge of murder, evidence was admissible of the conduct of the defendant towards others extending over many hours prior to the killing. Latham CJ said that the conduct was:

> "evidence of 'facts and matters which form constituent parts or ingredients of the transaction itself or explain or make intelligible the course of conduct pursued'".

Thus, in the present case each defendant was entitled to give evidence of the sexual activities of the complainant with each of the other defendants over several hours. In an appropriate case, the "transaction" may include the events of several days. This is likely to be the case where the complainant was part of a group of people who have gone away for a weekend or holiday together. Per Gleeson C.J. *Bull v R* [2000] HCA 24 at [63].

(e) *Dual purpose statements*

28–27   It must be brought home to the jury that a dual purpose statement cannot be used for a hearsay purpose (if no hearsay exception applies), but if this is done, the warning does not have to be repeated every time the evidence is mentioned for a legitimate purpose: *Vidal v The Queen* [2011] UKPC 12 at [24].

28–30   In *Horncastle v R* [2009] UKSC 14 at [35], Lord Phillips regarded s.117 and s.129 as alternative gateways to admissibility:

> "Other categories of hearsay are made admissible because, in the ordinary way, they are likely to be reliable. Business records are made admissible (by s.117 or, where a machine is involved, s.129) because, in the ordinary way, they are compiled by persons who are disinterested and, in the ordinary course of events, such statements are likely to be accurate".

If Lord Phillips meant to imply that business documents stored on a computer are only admissible via s.117, it is submitted that he was mistaken. For a further discussion of the relationship of s.117 and s.129 see R. Pattenden, "Machinespeak: Section 129 of the Criminal Justice Act 2003" [2010] Crim. L.R. 623.

(g) *The Boundaries of hearsay*

(iv) *"Implied assertion"*

28–45   The rationale for not treating implied assertions as hearsay is considered in *Per* Hughes LJ , *R v Twist* [2011] EWCAS Crim 1143, (2011) 175 J.P. 257 at [8].

On the impact of Criminal Justice Act 2003, s.115 on implied assertions, see D.   **28–45**
Birch, "Interpreting the New Concept of Hearsay" [2010] Camb L.J. 72.

For a recent example of reliance on implied non-assertive conduct (that of an inter-   **28–47**
preter) as evidence that a request was for breath samples was properly communicated
to a defendant charged with the offence of failing to supply specimens of breath for
analysis contrary to s.7(6) of the Road Traffic Act 1988, see *Bielecki v DPP* [2011]
EWHC 2245 (Admin).

(v) *Negative hearsay?*

R v Patel [1981] 3 All ER 94 and *R v Shone* (1982) 76 Cr.App. R. 72 were discussed   **28–50**
in *R v Leigh* [2010] EWHC 345 (Admin). Applying s.115 of the Criminal Justice Act
2003, the Divisional Court said that "if the significance of a record lies not in what it
says, but in what it does not say i.e. the fact that it says nothing", it is not adduced for
a hearsay purpose.

(vi) *Survey evidence*

Survey evidence may use representations of fact provided by the people surveyed,   **28–51**
for example, that they were present in a room in which a television was showing a particular advertisement. A factual representation like this (made by pressing a button)
was found to be hearsay in *Hansen Beverage Co v Bickfords (Aus) Pty Ltd* (2007) 75
I.P.R. 505 at [125]-[126].

5.—PROCEEDINGS IN WHICH THE HEARSAY RULE DOES NOT APPLY

For the position in sentencing confiscation proceedings see *R v Clipston* [2011]   **28–52**
EWCA Crim 446.

6.—REFORM

fn.367 See also the Irish Law Commission Report on Hearsay LRC CP 60–2010   **28–56**
[2010] IELRC CP60.

CHAPTER 29

HEARSAY IN CIVIL PROCEEDINGS

1.—INTRODUCTION

fn.1 For a recent discussion on this issue see the Irish Law Commission Report on **29–01**
Hearsay LRC CP 60–2010 [2010] IELRC CP60

3.—SAFEGUARDS: SECTIONS 2–4

The new Family Procedure Rules 2010 (SI 2010/2955), which came into effect on **29–05**
April 6, 2011, restrict the effect of s. 2(1) of the Civil Evidence Act 1995 Act in family
proceedings, by virtue of r. 23.3:

> "Section 2(1) of the Civil Evidence Act 1995 (duty to give notice of intention to rely on
> hearsay evidence) does not apply—
>
> (a) to evidence at hearings other than final hearings;
>
> (b) to an affidavit or witness statement which is to be used at the final hearing but which
> does not contain hearsay evidence; or
>
> (c) where the requirement is excluded by a practice direction."

In relation to domestic violence protection orders, rule 4 of the Magistrates' Courts
(Domestic Violence Protection Order Proceedings) Rules 2011 (SI 2011/1434) dis-
applies s. 2(1) of the 1995 Act.

The Proceeds of Crime Act 2002 ("the 2002 Act") takes an approach to hearsay evidence that is, most charitably, less that straightforward. This appears to be in large part
because the Act sits at the intersection of civil and criminal justice, and makes provision
for a number of different types of proceeding.[1] The general position would appear to be

---

[1] R. v Vincent Clipstone [2011] EWCA Crim 446; [2011] All ER (D) 58 (Mar), [50].

that the provisions of the Civil Evidence Act 1995 do not apply to confiscation proceedings.[2] In *Clipstone,* Lord Justice Gross held that s. 46(2) of the 2002 Act was provided expressly to apply ss. 2–4 of the 1995 Act to restraint proceedings,[3] because the 1995 Act does not otherwise apply to the main body of Pt. 2, which concerns confiscation orders.[4]

There are, however, further exceptions. Restraint proceedings under the 2002 Act are now further shaped by the Criminal Procedure Rules 2011, which dis-apply s.2(1).[5] In detention order proceedings,[6] sections 2 to 4 apply in their entirety, including seemingly s. 2(1).[7] In receivership proceedings,[8] the Criminal Procedure Rules 2011 expressly dis-apply s. 2(1) of the 1995 Act.[9] This is a curious dis-application because, if we accept the approach taken in *Clipstone*, there is no indication that s. 2(1), or any other section of the 1995 Act, would have apply in receivership proceedings.

7.—HEARSAY EVIDENCE: THE APPROACH OF THE COURTS

29–15   The Family courts exercise generally a wide discretion to admit hearsay evidence. The wardship court, for example, has a duty to investigate all of the relevant circumstances that may touch upon the ward's future welfare, and this includes considering anonymous evidence.[10]

---

[2] Sections. 6–39 of the 2002 Act. The hearsay provisions of the Criminal Justice Act 2003 also do not apply, and the approach taken is instead specific to the 2002 Act: 2011] EWCA Crim 446, at [61].

[3] Proceeds of Crime Act 2002, ss.40–47; s.2 of the Proceeds of Crime 2002 (Enforcement in different parts of the United Kingdom) Order 2002 (SI 2002/3133).

[4] [2011] EWCA Crim 446, at [50],

[5] Criminal Procedure Rules (SI 2011 / 1709), r.61.8.

[6] Proceedings for an order under section 47M of the Proceeds of Crime Act 2002 Act, or an appeal under section 47O, as amended by s.55(2) of the Policing and Crime Act 2009 (c.26).

[7] Section 47Q of the 2002 Act.

[8] Section 2 of the Proceeds of Crime 2002 (Enforcement in different parts of the United Kingdom) Order 2002 S.I.2002/3133, broadly ss.48–56 and 62–66 of the 2002 Act.

[9] Criminal Procedure Rules (S.I. 2011 / 1709), rule 61.8.

[10] Re T (Wardship: Impact of Police Intelligence) [2009] EWHC 2440 Fam; [2010] 1 FLR 1048, at [89] (McFarlane J). See also Chief Constable & Anor v YK & Ors [2010] EWHC 2438 (Fam), concerning the Forced Marriage (Civil Protection) Act 2007, where the court affirmed, at [18], that "There is, moreover, nothing in the Act to stop the court acting on hearsay evidence, or information provided to it by the police which has not been disclosed to the respondents."

CHAPTER 30

HEARSAY IN CRIMINAL PROCEEDINGS

1.—GENERAL

(a) *Scope of this Chapter*

It was held in *R v Clipston* [2011] EWCA Crim 446 that although sentencing con-   **30–01**
fiscation proceedings pursuant to the Proceeds of Crime At 2003 are proceedings of
a criminal character, the hearsay regime found in the Criminal Justice Act 2003 is
not strictly applicable. Instead, the provisions of the 2003 Act should be applied by
analogy, but flexibly. Gross L.J. said, ibid at [64]:

"What then is a Judge to do when faced with the proposed introduction of hearsay
evidence in the course of confiscation proceedings under Part 2 of POCA?... Plainly,
it cannot be that anything goes ... We cannot sensibly be unduly prescriptive but we
venture the following broad considerations:

i)   In many instances, there will or should be no realistic issue as to the *admissibility* of the evidence, not least given the focus of POCA on "information".

ii)   There will, however, be occasions where a hearsay statement is of importance
and seriously in dispute so that *admissibility* is, quite properly, a live issue. If
so, as it seems to us, the CJA 2003 regime, applied by analogy, will furnish the
most appropriate framework for adjudicating on such issues. The vital needs is
for the Judge in such a situation to understand the potential for unfairness and

[105]

to "borrow", as appropriate, from the available guidance in s.114(2) (together with the matters contained in s.116) of the CJA. However, when applying this regime – and especially the "interests of justice" test in s.114(1)(d) – it will be of the first importance to keep the post-conviction context in mind. There may well be room for more flexibility than in the trial context.

iii) In many cases, the real issue will be the *weight* rather than the *admissibility* of the evidence or information in question. If so, the "checklist" contained in s.114(2) (and the matters set out in s.116) of the CJA 2003, suitably adapted to address weight rather than admissibility, will here too provide a valuable (if not exhaustive)framework of reference. In any event and in every case, a Judge must of course proceed judicially, having regard to the limitations of the evidence or information under consideration (including by way of examples, the reliability of the maker, the circumstances in which it came to be made, the reason why oral evidence cannot be given and the absence of cross-examination). Furthermore, care must invariably be taken to ensure that the defendant has a proper opportunity to be heard.

iv) Here, as elsewhere in the sentencing process, the Judge will need to exercise judgment. In the present context, such judgment must be exercised consistently with both the legislative intention underpinning POCA and . . . the need for fairness to all concerned . . ."

2.—DEFINITION OF HEARSAY IN THE CRIMINAL JUSTICE ACT 2003

30–03   Hearsay is defined in s.114(1)(d) of the Criminal Justice Act 2003, as "a statement not made in oral evidence in the proceedings" that is adduced "as evidence of any matter stated". A court must answer four preliminary questions whenever evidence is challenged as hearsay in a criminal trial. First, is it relevant? Secondly, is it a "statement" within the meaning of s.114 (1) read in conjunction with s.115? Communication is not synonymous with "statement":

"If, for example, the communication does no more than ask a question, it is difficult to see how it contains any statement. A text message to someone asking "Will you have any crack tomorrow" seems to us to contain no statement at all."
Per Hughes L.J., *R v Twist* [2011] EWCA Crim 1143, (2011) 175 J.P. 257 at [15].

Once the court has decided that a communication contains a statement, the court must ask whether it is adduced to prove a stated fact (or opinion). If it is adduced to prove something else, such as the fact that the statement was made, the hearsay provisions of the 2003 Act have no application:

"Most (but not all) communications will no doubt contain one or more matters stated, but it does not always follow that any is the matter which the party seeking to adduce the communication is setting out to try to prove, i.e. that the communication is proffered as evidence of that matter. He may sometimes be trying to prove simply that two people were in communication with each other, and not be concerned with the content at all. On other occasions he may be trying to prove the relationship between the parties to the communication but not be in the least concerned with the veracity of the content of it. And there may, of course, be occasions where what he seeks to prove is that a matter stated in the communications is indeed fact. The opening words of section 114 show that it is the last of these situations which engages the rules against hearsay." Per Hughes LJ , *R v Twist* [2011] EWCA Crim 1143, (2011) 175 J.P. 257 at [6].

The fourth and final question is whether one of the purposes (not necessarily the only or dominant purpose) for which the stated fact (or opinion) was made was to make another person believe the stated fact (or opinion) (s.115(3)(a)).

Since the purpose s.115 (3) requires the maker of the statement to have must be to make *another* person believe or act upon the stated fact (or opinion), a statement that is not addressed to someone else, such as an entry in a secret diary, is not hearsay. D. Birch, "Interpreting the New Concept of Hearsay" [2010] Camb L.J. 72 points out that if the diary is that of the defendant and contains a confession of guilt, the requirements of s.76 of the Police and Criminal Evidence Act 1984 might have to be satisfied because a confession in a secret diary falls within the definition of a confession in s.82(1). It is hard to imagine a situation in which this would present difficulties for the prosecution.

The purpose requirement in s.115(3) has the further consequence that if the stated fact is known by the maker of the statement to be believed already by the recipient, the statement is not hearsay because in these circumstances it is not likely to be any part of the maker's purpose in making the statement to induce the recipient to believe the fact. Suppose, for example, A says to B, "Is C here? He is my dealer". The express assertion that A and C have a buyer-seller relationship will be hearsay only if A is in some doubt as to whether B is aware of this fact already. In *R v Elliott* [2010] EWCA Crim 2378 the Court of Appeal held that letters sent to the defendant in prison that contained references to the defendant's membership of a gang were not hearsay evidence of the fact of his gang membership because the letters had not been written for the purpose of causing the defendant to believe that he was a gang member or to act on the basis that the fact that he was a gang member was true.

The same communication may sometimes be hearsay and sometimes not, depending on why it is adduced, see e.g. *R v Mullings* [2010] EWCA Crim 2820 at [20] and D. Birch, "Interpreting the New Concept of Hearsay" [2010] Cam. L.J.72. The defendant in *R v Leonard* [2009] EWCA Crim 1251 received text messages that commented upon the quality or quantity of the drugs. The Crown relied upon the comments about the quality and quantity of past drug supplies to prove that the defendant was a drug dealer. This was a hearsay use of the text messages because the senders of the messages had intended the defendant to believe what they had to say about the quality and quantity of the drugs. In *R v Twist supra* at [24] Hughes LJ said that:

> "[i]t would clearly have been different if the Crown had relied on the messages not to prove the quality of past supplies (and though this route that the defendant was a dealer) but merely to show that the relationship between the parties was one of drug customer and drug supplier, without any attempt to prove the quality of the past supplies."

In *R v Twist supra*, on the other hand, and in the earlier case of *R v Chrysostomou* [2010] EWCA Crim 1403, the drugs were adduced for a non-hearsay purpose. Aikens L.J. explained in *Chrysostomou* (at [28]) that:

> ". . . the purpose for which the Crown wished to adduce the texts in evidence was not to prove, as fact, any matters stated in those texts. The object of adducing them was as evidence of an underlying state of affairs, which was the basis on which "John"

apparently sent the texts to the appellant, viz. that the appellant dealt with drugs and so could meet John's demands."

The upshot of the text message cases is that when a communication is offered as evidence, there is no hearsay issue unless the person who made the statement made it *for the purpose of being believed or acted upon as being true*. In *R v Lowe* [2011] EWCA Crim 1143, (2011) 175 J.P. 257 the defendant had sent text messages to the complainant in which he had admitted raping her. These messages were held not to be hearsay when offered by the prosecution as evidence that the defendant had raped the complainant because "the defendant, when sending them, did not have as one of his purposes to cause the complainant to believe that she had been raped" (ibid at [42]). The complainant knew and believed this fact already. (If the messages had been classified as hearsay, they would nevertheless have been admissible under the confession exception as to which see Police and Criminal Evidence Act 1984, s.76).

30–04   In *R v Twist* ibid at [16] Hughes L.J. stressed that for a statement to be hearsay it is not enough that a speaker intends the hearer to act on a matter stated. Crucially, the speaker must wish "the hearer to act upon the basis that a *matter stated in the message is as stated (i.e. true)*". In *R v Boothman* an appeal heard at the same time as *R v Twist*, the defendant had received orders for drugs by text message, some of which alluded to cocaine. Hughes L.J. said (at [32]):

">. . . The fact sought to be proved was that the defendant was dealing in cocaine, as well as in cannabis. That was a highly relevant fact. There were representations (statements) to that effect in some of the messages, and others carried that meaning. But in none of the messages did the sender have it as one of his purposes to make the defendant believe that he was a supplier of cocaine, or to act on the basis that that representation was true. They no doubt wanted him to act on their orders, but that . . . is not the same thing as wanting him to accept the truth of their references to his cocaine dealing . . . "If a statement is made to a machine, by parity of reasoning, one of the purposes of making the statement must have been to have the machine act on the statement *as a true statement of fact*.

30–05   In *R v Twist* ibid at [13] Hughes L.J. used hypothetical examples to show that s.114 in conjunction with s.115 excludes an "implied assertion" (a difficult concept that is best avoided *ibid* at [19]) from the scope of the hearsay rule:

">. . . If a buyer for a large chain store telephones the sales director of a manufacturer, with whom he routinely does business, and orders a supply of breakfast cereal or fashion jeans he is generally not representing as a fact or matter either (a) that the sales director's firm manufactures the flakes or the jeans or (b) that he the buyer works for the chain store. Crucially for the application of the Act, even if it be suggested that the order should be construed as an "implied assertion" of either fact (a) or fact (b), it will be beyond doubt in most cases that the caller does not have it as one of his purposes to cause the recipient to believe or act upon either of those facts. The recipient knows them very well. Those are simply the facts (or matters) which are common knowledge as between the parties to the call. Neither is, therefore, a matter stated in the call for the purpose of sections 114 and 115. The call is however evidence of both fact (a) and fact (b). It is not, no doubt, conclusive, at least if there is any realistic possibility of mistake, but it is undoubtedly evidence of those facts. Conversely, if the caller tells the recipient, perhaps in order to induce him to speed up the supply, that the buyers have already sold 5 tons of the goods, it is his purpose to induce the recipient to believe that fact. If that were the fact sought to be proved, the call would be hearsay evidence of that matter . . ."

A further hypothetical scenario (ibid at [14]) makes the point that conduct that is not intended to communicate a fact is not a statement and therefore incapable of constituting hearsay:

". . . If there is a queue of young people outside a building at midnight, obviously waiting for an evening out, that is some evidence tending to prove that the building is being operated as a club, which may be the matter which it is sought to prove, perhaps in licensing proceedings. There is no statement of that matter for the purposes of the Act."

Building on this hypothetical scenario, Hughes L.J. gave another example of the distinction between a statement that is hearsay and an implied assertion that is not:

". . . If several of the queuers were heard to be telling others about last week's 'rave', the only way that could possibly be regarded as a statement of the fact that this was a club would be by treating it, artificially as it seems to us, as an implied assertion of that fact. But it makes no difference whether it is so treated or not, because none of the speakers would have the purpose of inducing any listener to believe or to act upon the fact that the place is a club, since that is simply a common basis for conversation, and all of them know it. Conversely, if the issue is not whether the place was a club, but rather whether there was a large event the previous week, the statement of the fact/matter that there had been such an event would indeed be caught by the hearsay rule; those who spoke of it were doing so with the purpose of inducing their hearers who had not been there to believe it. The out of court statement would indeed be hearsay evidence of that matter . . ."

If a fact implied by a communication was not implied for the purpose of either causing belief in that fact by another or another person to act on the basis that the implied fact is true, admissibility of that communication as evidence of that which it implies depends solely on its relevance to a matter in issue (ibid at [20]). If admitted, the communication is not conclusive evidence of the implied fact:

"To take an example, a single message requesting the supply of drugs, or for that matter a gun, might have been misdirected by mistake, or might be based on a mistaken belief that the recipient is likely to be able to supply what is asked for. No doubt, the more similar messages there are, sent independently of one another, the more likely it is that they do prove the fact alleged, but that will depend on what possible alternative explanations there might be for the evidence. Whether a communication which is not hearsay does or does not prove the fact alleged is always a matter of weight for the jury." Per Hughes L.J. *ibid* at [21].

In *R v Chrysostomou* [2010] EWCA Crim 1403 the defendant received text messages that implied that he dealt in drugs, for example, "I need 7g will you do it for 200". This text message (and others like it) was adduced by the prosecution as evidence of his bad character. On appeal the admissibility of this evidence was challenged inter alia on the grounds that the evidence was hearsay. Adopting the approach of the minority in *R v Kearley* [1992] 2 A.C. 228, the Court of Appeal treated the emails as circumstantial evidence that the defendant dealt in drugs. A more satisfactory analysis of why the messages did not offend the hearsay rule was offered by Hughes L.J. in *R v Twist supra.* The messages were relied on to prove what they implied viz. that the defendant dealt in drugs. It was not the purpose of the person sending the texts to cause the defendant to believe he was a drug dealer or to act on this as a true fact, ergo the implicit statement that the defendant was a drug dealer was not hearsay.

On the impact of Criminal Justice Act 2003, s.115 on implied assertions, see D. Birch, "Interpreting the New Concept of Hearsay" [2010] Camb L.J. 72.

30–05b   The omission of a statement is not hearsay. In *R v Leigh* [2010] EWHC 345 (Admin) the defendant was charged with failing to provide information relating to the driver of a vehicle, as required by the Road Traffic Act 1988, s.172(2). An official gave evidence as to how a response to a request for information is routinely dealt with and that there was no record of a response having been received from the defendant. Disagreeing with the District judge, Elias J. held that this evidence was not hearsay. The prosecution did not rely on the record for the purpose of establishing a matter stated in it. The significance of the record lay in the fact that nothing was stated in the record, from which it could be inferred that no response had been received. This evidence fell outside s.115.

3.—OVERVIEW OF THE CRIMINAL JUSTICE ACT 2003

30–06   No question of admitting hearsay under an exception to the hearsay rule recognized in s.114 arises unless the tendered statement is relevant which depends on the facts of the case: *R v Twist* [2011] EWCAS Crim 1143, (2011) 175 J.P. 257 at [11].

30–11   Criminal Procedure Rules 2011, Part 34 (and associated Practice Direction) requires formal notice to be given to the court and the other party of an intention to introduce hearsay evidence under Criminal Justice Act, 2003 s.114(1)(d) (evidence admissible in the interests of justice, s.116 (evidence of an unavailable witness) and s.121 (multiple hearsay), but not if it is to be introduced under some other section such as, for example, s.117 (business etc. records). The notice period for the prosecutor is not less than 14 days after the defendant pleaded guilty and for the defendant as soon as reasonably practicable. A notice of opposition to hearsay is required regardless of whether formal notice of the intention to produce the hearsay is required.

On the necessity to observe the notice rules if a hearsay statement is tendered during sentencing after the guilty plea see *R v Lima* [2010] EWCA Crim 284.

On the necessity for leave if notice is not given, see *R v Warren* [2010] EWCA Crim 3267 at [8].

If the prosecution and defence agree to a statement being read at the trial on the factual basis that the witness has deliberately disappeared in order to avoid testifying, it is not open to the defence to argue that the statement was inadmissible on appeal because there was insufficient evidence that the witness had not attended deliberately and that reasonable steps had been taken to find him: *R v Lyons* [2010] EWCA Crim 2029.

4.—ADMITTING HEARSAY BY CONSENT

Where the parties agree before the trial opens that hearsay evidence is to be put **30–12** before the jury by agreement, the court must be informed of this at the outset of the trial. If an agreement is made during the trial, the judge should be told immediately after the agreement. This gives the judge the opportunity to consider the timing and manner of putting the evidence before the jury and the directions of law that are needed in the summing up: *R v DJ* [2010] EWCA Crim 385.

The admission of social security files that relate to someone other than the defendant requires judicial approval, even if the parties are agreed that the material be seen by the jury.

"... This is because the documents held by social services are generally subject to public interest immunity and the rights both of the social services and of the persons who are the subject of the documentation must be respected." (ibid at [20] per Thomas L.J

The judge's job is to balance the respective interests. One thing the judge will have to consider is whether redactions are needed.

5.—UNAVAILABLE WITNESS

(c) *Statutory requirements for admissibility*

(iii) *Reasons for unavailability that result in admissibility of an out-of-court statement without leave*

In *R v Evans* [2010] EWCA Crim 2516 at [18] the Court of Appeal accepted that as a **30–19** result of the Supreme Court's decision in *Horncastle v R* [2009] UKSC 14, a statement by a dead witness is not admissible unless either demonstrably reliable or its reliability can be properly tested and assessed. It concluded that the second condition was satisfied. The same point was made about the evidence of another witness who had agreed to give evidence by video link from Spain but had failed to show up on the appointed day. The Court of Appeal upheld the trial judge's decision to admit evidence she had given earlier that year to a Spanish magistrate in response to a letter of request and six years earlier on commission in Gibraltar notwithstanding that she had never been cross-examined because there jury were in a position to test and assess her evidence.

A decision to admit the statement of a witness who was living in North Cyprus under s.116(2)(c) was upheld in *R v Deakin* [2009] EWCA Crim 2541 at [14] because the police had taken all reasonable steps to secure the attendance of the witness. In this case, this witness had given evidence and been cross-examined in an earlier trial involving the same defendants and allegations. In *Brett v DPP* [2009] EWHC 440 (Admin) the defence served notice pursuant to s.16(4) of the Road Traffic Offenders Act 1988 requiring the analysis who had prepared a blood analysis certificate to attend court. The analyst was out of the country so the Deputy District Judge admitted the certificate under s.116. This decision was upheld in the Divisional Court.

A witness who deliberately puts himself in a position where he cannot be found because he does not wish to give evidence is within the scope of s.116(2)(d) and outside the scope of s.116(5): *R v Lyons* [2010] EWCA Crim 2029 at [14].

(iv) *Unavailability that result in admissibility of an out-of-court statement with leave: declarant does not give evidence through fear*

30–21 In *R v Sullivan* [2010] EWCA Crim 2676 the Court of Appeal said that the requirements of s.114(2)(e) can be satisfied without the witness stating in express terms that he is unwilling to give evidence from fear. In this case, the witness's fear was demonstrated by the change in his demeanour in videos make before and after he had allegedly been threatened.

In *Horncastle v R* [2009] UKSC 14 at [68] Lord Phillips said:

> ". . . One situation where Strasbourg has recognized that there is justification for not calling a witness to give evidence at the trial . . . is where the witness is so frightened of the personal consequences if he gives evidence . . . that he is not prepared to do so. If the defendant is responsible for the fear, then fairness demands that he should not profit from its consequences. Even if he is not, the reality may be that the prosecution are simply not in a position to prevail on the witness to give evidence. In such circumstances, having due regard for the human rights of the witness or the victim, as well as those of the defendant, fairness may well justify reading the statement of the witness . . ."

(v) *Multiple (compound) hearsay*

30–24 Section 121 was relied on in *R v Thakrar* [2010] EWCA Crim 1505. One of the appellants was arrested in Northern Cyprus where he had flown the day after a multiple murder. The Northern Cypriot police took written statements from three witnesses who stated in them that the appellant had boasted to them of having committed the murders with his brother. The appellant had used an interpreter to communicate to two of the witnesses. None of the witnesses was willing to come to the United Kingdom from Northern Cyprus to give evidence at the trial either or to give evidence by live video link, so s.116(2)(c) applied, but the statements were also either second-hand or (where an English-Turkish interpreter was used) third-hand hearsay. After hearing evidence from the North Cypriot police officer who took the statements were taken, the trial judge allowed the prosecution to put the three statements before the jury. The Court of Appeal said that the value of the statements was considerable and that there was every reason to regard them as reliable as they reported details known only to eyewitnesses to the murders and neither the witnesses nor the Northern Cypriot police had a motive to invent the admissions. This meant that it was in the interests of justice to give the leave required by s.121(1)(c) to introduce multiple hearsay.

6.—BUSINESS AND SIMILAR DOCUMENTS

(a) *Introduction*

30–27 For further analysis see "Machinespeak: Section 129 of the Criminal Justice Act 2003" [2010] Crim LR 623.

8.—Rebutting Alleged Fabrication of Evidence

For an analysis of *R v Athwal* [2009] EWCA Crim 789 and its shortcomings, see R.   **30–33**
Pattenden "R v Athwal" (2009) E & P 342 and R. Munday, "Athwal and All That:
Previous Statements, Narrative, and the Taxonomy of Hearsay" (2010) 74 Journal of
Criminal Law 415.

9.—Forgotten Information

As well as considering the factors listed in s.114(2), in *R v Burton* [2011]   **30–35**
EWCA Crim 1990, a prosecution for sexual activity with a child who refused to come
to court or make a statement, the Court of Appeal took the following factors into
account:

1. The complainant harboured a degree of affection for the defendant and was,
    therefore, likely to support the defence contention that there had been no sexual
    contact;

2. If she were forced to testify, whether for the prosecution or defence, and denied
    a sexual relationship with the defendant, her statement could be likely to be
    admissible as a prior inconsistent statement;

3. It was irrelevant that the defence did not want to call the complainant as a
    witness because it did not want to run any risk that she might confirm the
    existence of a sexual relationship ("A criminal trial is not a game" *ibid* at
    [17]).

4. It was unwise to compel a reluctant witness of "tender years" to testify.

5. The out-of-court statement was neither the sole nor decisive evidence against the
    defendant. It added nothing to what the defendant had admitted to the police,
    at the same time, it was right for the jury to be informed of the complainant's
    immediate reaction to the discovery of her possession of pregnancy testing kits
    and love letters from the defendant.

Burnton L.J. described the case as "exceptional" (*ibid* at [15]).

10.—Recent Complaint

The Coroners and Justice Act 2009, Sch.23(3) para.1, which came into effect on   **30–36**
April 6, 2010, repealed Criminal Justice Act 2003, s.120(7)(d) making it unnecessary
for a complaint to be recent.

fn.270 See R v Ashraf A [2011] EWCA Crim 1517, where the Court confirmed that
the direction in R v AA [2007] Crim 1779 should routinely be given where evidence is
addressed under s.120(7) CJA 2003.

12.—Inclusionary Discretion

30–44   The Supreme Court's confidence in *Horncastle v R* [2009] UKSC 14 that the Criminal Justice Act 2003 has sufficient safeguards for a conviction founded to a decisive degree or solely on hearsay to be safe rings hollow if judges are readily able to circumvent the Criminal Justice Act 2003's hearsay code by relying on the inclusionary discretion found in s.114(1)(d). Unsurprisingly, Lord Phillips (*ibid* at [31]) described the discretion as "a limited residual power" and in *R v Twist* [2011] EWCA Crim 1143, (2011) 175 J.P. 257, Hughes L.J. said (*ibid* at [22]) that admission of hearsay under s.114(1)(d):

> ". . . [i]s not routine, nor a matter of mere form; it requires careful thought, having due regard to (especially) reliability and the opportunity to test it; . . ."

A cautious approach to the discretionary admittance of hearsay statements is evident also in the judgments in *R v ED* [2010] EWCA Crim 1213, *R v CW* [2010] EWCA Crim 72 and *R v M* [2011] EWCA Crim 2341. In *R v M* the hearsay evidence consisted of the recording of a 999 call by the complainant and her witness statement. The judge admitted the evidence. The Court of Appeal concluded that in doing so the judge had failed to place proper weight on the matters listed in s.114 (1), and the consideration of the factor is 2.114(2)(g) was flawed. In *Ed*, an historic sex abuse case, the Court of Appeal disapproved of the trial judge's decision to use s.114(1)(d) to admit hearsay evidence from an school friend of one of the victims of a complaint made nearer the time of the offence. The trial judge had failed to take into account the fact that the prosecution was at fault in not giving the witness enough notice that she would be required to give oral evidence. She had been notified less than a month before the trial by which time she already had a holiday booked with her partner and children. Given the fact that she was then six months pregnant and very distressed about the prospect of cancelling the holiday, the prosecution had elected not to call her to testify. The Court emphasized that s.114(1)(d) should not be used to circumvent s.114(a)–(c).

In *R v CW*, another historic sex abuse case, there was compelling medical evidence that C, the victim, had been sexually abused. The live issue was who had done it. S, who had adopted the victim when she was six years old, was allowed to testify about disclosures C had made to her over a number of years about what she had suffered at the hands of CW. This hearsay evidence confirmed the oral testimony of an eyewitness to C's abuse. The Court of Appeal criticized the trial judge for not scrutinizing with sufficient care why it was suggested that C should not be called as a witness. Williams J. said (ibid at [41]-[44]) that:

> ". . . at the time this application was made to the judge C was aged fifteen. Obviously there was no reason relating to her age why she could not give oral evidence at court. We appreciate, of course, that S appeared to have strongly held and genuine views that giving evidence at a criminal trial would have a detrimental impact upon C's wellbeing. So far as we can judge, however, no particular steps were taken to ascertain whether S's views were correct. No request was made to her to permit an examination of C by a suitably qualified professional. All that occurred was that a police officer or police officers discussed with her the desirability of C giving evidence. Neither

the prosecuting authorities nor the learned judge took steps to test S's resolve. She was not asked to make a statement dealing specifically and in detail with the reasons why she objected to C giving evidence. She was not asked to give evidence before the learned judge to explain why she objected to C giving evidence. The position seems to have been, throughout, that the prosecuting authorities accepted that S, in effect, had the right to decide whether or not C gave evidence. No one from the prosecuting authorities took any steps towards asking C directly what she felt about giving evidence. We appreciate that the authorities would wish to act with a degree of caution and that S was, apparently, preventing anyone from speaking directly with C. Nonetheless, we find it hard to accept that a suitably qualified professional could not have persuaded S that it was appropriate for C to be spoken to directly about the issue of giving evidence—or at least that a suitably qualified professional should not have been appointed to make the attempt. We have reached the conclusion that in the circumstances presented to the learned judge he should not have admitted the hearsay evidence of S. Further, the learned judge was wrong to maintain his ruling . . . when he had received an indication that C might be prepared to give evidence. At the very least . . . the judge should have directed that steps be taken to ascertain C's true view before he reached a concluded view upon whether the hearsay evidence should be admitted."

Additionally, the trial judge had failed to pay sufficient attention to the difficulty of assessing C's reliability or for the defendant of challenging C's out-of-court statements.

Not every recent appeal has succeeded. In *R v Seton* [2010] EWCA Crim 450 the witness was a criminal serving a life sentence for murder. At a late stage, the appellant had alleged that the witness had also committed the murder with which the appellant was charged. After learning of this accusation, the witness had indignantly denied his involvement to his wife and son in telephone calls from prison. The prison authorities had tape-recorded these calls. Since the witness refused to give evidence for the prosecution at the appellant's trial, application was made to the trial judge to admit the tape-recordings. After considering the factors listed in s.114(2), the trial judge had agreed to this because, in his opinion, the evidence was strongly probative. The defence was able to point out to the jury that what the witness had said to his wife and son was self-serving, and that the witness was a serious criminal who knew his calls were being recorded. The judge's decision was upheld by the Court of Appeal, which did not think it necessary for the prosecution to bring the witness to court and demonstrate his unwillingness to testify.

In *R v Kamahl Forde* [2010] EWCA Crim 2250 an unknown woman handed police a piece of paper with the registration number of the car used by the people who had fired two shots at a house. This hearsay evidence was crucial to the prosecution's case. The Court of Appeal followed *R v Mayers* [2008] EWCA Crim 2989 and held that the only gateway for admitting anonymous evidence is the Criminal Evidence (Witness Anonymity) Act 2008, which did not apply. See also *R v Fox* [2010] EWCA Crim 1280. The 2008 Act has been repealed and evidence by anonymous witnesses is now dealt with in the Coroners and Justice Act 2009.

It is arguable that Parliament did not intend to forbid out-of-court statements by unidentified persons under all of the exceptions to the hearsay rule recognized in the 2003 Act (including surviving common law exceptions) and Hughes L.J. seems to have recognized this in *R v Twist* [2011] EWCA Crim 1143, (2011) 175 J.P. 257 when he remarked that:

". . . whilst there may be some forms of anonymous hearsay which are nevertheless admissible, such as business records or the statement of an unidentified agent of the defendant, the hearsay testimony of an anonymous witness may well fail the interests of justice test of admissibility; an example is *Fox* [2010] EWCA Crim 1280 where the contents of an anonymous 999 call were inadmissible as evidence that the facts reported were true."

In fact, the Law Commission envisaged the admissibility of statements by an unidentified declarant under s.114(1)(d) (see Law Commission, *Evidence in Criminal Proceedings: Hearsay and Related Topics* Cmnd No. 245 (1997) para.8.1430) . That report, of course, was written long before the House of Lords expressed its disapproval of anonymous witnesses in *R v Davies* [2008] UKHL 36, [2008] 1 A.C. 1128 (see 11–49 ante). In *Horncastle v R* [2009] UKSC14, [2010] 2 A.C. 373 Annexe 4 at [13] Lord Judge refused to distinguish between witnesses whose identity is withheld from the jury or whose identity is simply unknown. However, as Ormerod points out in a commentary to *Ford* ([2011] Crim LR 475), *Horncastle* was concerned with whether admitting hearsay that is the sole or decisive evidence of guilt is compatible with Article 6. Lord Judge's endorsement of *R v Mayers supra* is therefore *obiter*. Ormerod also points out that "witness" is defined narrowly in s.97 of the Coroners and Justice Act 2009 as a "person called, or proposed to be called, to give evidence at the trial". It is a strained interpretation to include amongst the "proposed" witnesses, a witness whose identity is not known. The commentary goes on to note the risk that if "witness" is narrowly interpreted, the need to obtain an anonymous witness order could be circumvented by a witness refusing to divulge his or her identity. The greater risk, however, is surely that the prosecution will not do enough to identify the witness.

If the maker of the statement does not have to be identified for admissibility under s.117 (as Hughes L.J. presupposes in *Twist supra*), could this section have been used to admit the note with the car registration number that was held inadmissible in *R v Kamahl Forde supra*? Probably not: the person who handed the note to the police might not have had personal knowledge of the registration number and, as an intermediary, might not have satisfied s.117(2)(a).

30–47 On the use of a confession by D1 as evidence against D2, a co-defendant, see also *R v Thakrar* [2010] EWCA Crim 1505, which is discussed further at para.31–38.

13.—OTHER STATUTES

(h) *Other documentary evidence*

30–59 It was held in *West Midlands Probation Board v French* [2008] EWHC 2631(Admin), [2009] 1 W.L.R. 1715 that a copy of a licence issued by the governor of a prison pursuant to Criminal Justice Act 1991, s.40A was an "order" within the meaning of Documentary Evidence Act 1868, s2 and therefore admissible under s.114(1)(a) of the Criminal Justice Act 2003

14.—Common Law Categories of Admissibility

(h) *Other documentary evidence*

It was held in *R v Phillips* [2010] EWCA Crim 378 that attribution of surname   **30–62**
by reputation is permitted by s.118(1) rule 3(c). In this case, the witness was able to
identify the defendant from personal knowledge, but had to rely on information from
others to refer to him by his correct surname when making the identification. The
court noted that very few people know a person's surname at first hand.

15.—General Powers to Control Admission of Hearsay Evidence

(a) *Discretionary exclusion of prima facie admissible hearsay*

In *R v Horncastle v R* [2009] UKSC 14 at [36] Lord Phillips interpreted s.126 as a   **30–66**
confirmation of:

"the general power of the judge (which existed at common law and is enshrined in s.78
of the Police and Criminal Evidence Act 1984) to exclude any evidence relied upon
by the Crown (but not by a defendant) if its admission would have such an adverse
effect on the fairness of the trial that it ought not to be admitted."

Additionally, the section imposed a:

"further obligation upon the judge to exclude hearsay evidence if its admission would
generate satellite disputes which would cause an undue waste of time such as to out-
weigh the case for admitting it."

His words support a broad interpretation of s.126.
   fn.415 See R v Atkinson [2011] EWCA Crim 1796 where the Court, upholding the
decision of the trial judge not to admit the evidence under s.116(2)(d), stated that the
considerations under s.114(1)(d) were roughly the same as those under s.126(1)(b).

(b) *Stopping case because of unconvincing hearsay*

Section 125 was referred to in *R v Evans* [2010] EWCA Crim 2516 at [27] but   **30–69**
nothing of significance was said.
   In *Horncastle v R* [2009] UKSC 14 at [36] Lord Phillips said that s.125 is an important exception to the usual rule that assessment of the weight of evidence is exclusively
for the jury.

16.—Procedural Matters

(c) *Warning the jury*

30–75   In *R v Evans* [2010] EWCA Crim 2516 at [26] the Court of Appeal said that if a statement by an absent witness is read to the court, it is the judge's duty to warn the jury of the inherent weaknesses of hearsay evidence and to draw jurors' attention to doubts about the reliability and/or integrity of the maker of the statement. There is no further obligation to direct the jury as to whether the hearsay evidence is reliable or not.

A warning is not necessary if there is no issue between the prosecution and defence about the accuracy of the hearsay evidence that has been admitted: *R v Curtis* [2010] EWCA Crim 1778 at [17].

When hearsay is admitted for the defence, the judge must make it clear to the jury that the statements are relied on for the truth of their contents: *R v DJ* [2010] EWCA Crim 385 at [29]

In *R v Horncastle v R* [2009] UKSC 14 at [38] Lord Phillips said that a judge ahs to direct the jury on the dangers of relying on hearsay evidence.

17.—Hearsay and the European Convention on Human Rights

30–80   The Supreme Court in *Horncastle v R* [2009] UKSC 14 endorsed the judgment of the Court of Appeal in *R v Horncastle* [2009] EWA Crim 964 (which it described as "complementary") except in one particular: it disagreed that anonymous and absent witnesses should be treated differently:

> ". . . Each situation results in a potential disadvantage to the defendant. The extent of that disadvantage will depend on the facts of the particular case. I cannot see why a sole or decisive test should apply in the case of anonymous evidence but not in the case of a witness statement." Per Lord Phillips *ibid* at [50]

Whether evidence or is likely to be the sole or decisive evidence is *relevant* to the question of whether the court should permit it to be given anonymously but there is no mandatory rule prohibiting the admission of such evidence. Likewise, the hearsay exceptions recognized in the Criminal Justice Act 2003 are not subject to a mandatory "sole or decisive" test. The hearsay regime in the 2003 Act is a carefully crafted code that contains safeguards that make such a test unnecessary.

Art.6(3)(d) does not mention the sole or decisive test and the only rationale the Supreme Court could discern for it is to avoid an unsafe conviction because of unreliable evidence. Paradoxically, the test requires the exclusion of hearsay evidence that is both compelling and decisive. For example, the sole witness to a hit and run accident in which a cyclist is killed gives the police the registration number of the vehicle responsible and shortly afterwards dies. The police find that the vehicle corresponding to the registration number and its owner match the descriptions supplied by the eyewitness and the owner declines to answer questions about his whereabouts at the time of the accident. The test also creates severe practical difficulties if applied to English criminal procedure:

"The judge will have to rule inadmissible any witness statement capable of proving 'decisive'. This will be no easy task . . . If 'decisive' means capable of making the difference between a finding of guilty and innocence, then all hearsay evidence will have to be excluded." Per Lord Phillips, *ibid* at [90]

In the Supreme Court's opinion, in *Al-Khawaja* the ECtHR misread the relevant Strasbourg jurisprudence and failed to distinguish continental and common law criminal procedure. The right of confrontation that Art.6(3)(d) is an instrumental right directed at an aspect of a fair trial that continental criminal procedure had failed to address:

"The reports of the Strasbourg cases show that evidence given during the instruction by witnesses whom the defendant had had no chance to question was frequently used at the trial. There was no bar to the reception of hearsay evidence nor rules of admissibility designed to prevent the tribunal at the trial from receiving evidence on the ground that its prejudicial effect outweighed its probative value." Per Lord Phillips at [60].

The Art.6(3)(d) right is not absolute: Strasbourg has recognized that in the interests of justice there are circumstances that justify the admission of statements of witnesses who have not been subjected to a confrontation with the defendant. The inability to examine the maker of a statement tendered by the prosecution does not necessarily make a trial is unfair. Unfairness has to be assessed on a case-by-case basis. In almost all cases in which the ECtHR has invoked the sole or decisive rule, application of the hearsay rules found in the Criminal Justice Act 2003 would have produced the same result. In a common law jurisdiction that has no judicial investigation, the regime for admitting statements by unavailable witnesses enacted in the Criminal Justice Act 2003 strikes the right balance between the defendant's absolute right to a fair trial and the interests of victims and society in conviction of the guilty.

Al-Khawaja and Taney has been re-argued before the Grand Chamber, but the judgment has not yet been handed down. It is by no means certain that the Grand Chamber will side with the UK Government and the Supreme Court. The Grand Chamber may not see the exclusion of unreliable evidence as the purpose of Art.6(3) (d). Rather, it may see the Article in terms of process values: the right to confront someone who formally accuses you of the crime charged. If so, it will not be enough for admissibility that the evidence is demonstrably reliable or, failing this, that the defence is in a position to test its reliability adequately during the trial. If this should be the Grand Chamber's response, it is important to appreciate that *Al-Khawaja and Taney* and earlier Strasbourg jurisprudence were concerned with statements offered by the prosecution and made for the purposes of a criminal investigation or prosecution. *Al-Khawaja* does not require exclusion of all hearsay that is the sole or decisive evidence against the defendant. For many out-of-court statements by unavailable witnesses, the relevant rules governing admissibility are comprehensively stated in the Criminal Justice Act 2003. Where an out-of-court statement was made as part of the criminal process and is tendered by the prosecutor, the trial judge will have to go beyond the requirements of the 2003 Act and assess its probable impact, if admitted. If "decisive" means "determinative" (in the sense that a reasonable jury could be satisfied of the defendant's guilt to the criminal standard on this evidence alone), this will not present insuperable difficulties.

Articles discussing *Horncastle v R* include W. O'Brien, "Confrontation: The

Defiance of the English Courts" University of Warwick Legal Studies Research Paper No. 2010–09 available http://papers.ssrn.com/sol3/papers.cfm?abstract_id=1598241; M. Requa, 'Absent witnesses and the UK Supreme Court: judicial deference s judicial dialogue?' (2010) 14 E & P 208; I. Jones, 'A Political judgment?' Reconciling hearsay and the right to challenge. (2010) 14 E&P 232-252. See also, I. Dennis, 'The Right to Confront Witnesses' [2010] Crim LR 255.

In *R v Evans* [2010] EWCA Crim 2516 counsel argued that as a result of the Supreme Court's decision in *Horncastle* hearsay evidence is inadmissible unless it is demonstrably reliable or its reliability can be properly tested and assessed. Without discussing whether this was correct, the Court of Appeal found that the evidence to which counsel objected was admissible because it could be properly tested or assessed without the opportunity to cross-examine the maker of the statement.

CHAPTER 31

RES GESTAE AND CERTAIN OTHER EXCEPTIONS TO THE HEARSAY RULE IN CRIMINAL PROCEEDINGS

2.—Sponteneous (Excited) Utterances

(e) *R. v Andrews*

The Ackner criteria laid down in *R v Andrews* were held on appeal to have been satisfied in *R v Spence* [2011] EWCA Crim 94 at [7]-[11].   **31–18**

5.—Admissions, Confessions and Mixed Statements

In *R v Thakrar* [2010] EWCA Crim 1505 statements by unavailable witnesses were admitted under s.116(1)(c) in conjunction with s.121(1)(c). The latter (s. 121(1)(c)) was relevant because the witnesses were reporting confessions by an appellant. The confessions not only incriminated the appellant, but also his brother and co-defendant. Stanley Burnton L.J. said (at [53]) that the Court of Appeal could not see: **31–38**

> "... any justification for excluding that part of Miran's confessions that incriminated his brother. If Miran did confess or boast as described in the statements, it is impossible to see why he should have falsely incriminated his brother if in fact someone else was his accomplice. It follows that the reliability of that part of his confession was as high, and the evidence given [the brother's] defence as valuable, as that part that incriminated Miran himself. The suggestion that [the brother] should have had a separate trial is unreal ... In any event, we do not accept the premise ... that if [the brother] had been tried alone, Miran's confession statements would not have been admitted in evidence."

There is no reference in the judgment to Police and Criminal Evidence Act 1984, s.76 or s.76A. In so far as the appellant's reported statements were confessions, this is likely to have been because the defence did not represent, and the court had no reason to think, that they were inadmissible under s.76. In so far as they incriminated the appellant's brother, the judgment implies that the common law rule that a confession is admissible only against its maker does not preclude the use of a confession against another person incriminated in it provided that s.76 is not a bar and the statement falls within an exception to the hearsay rule recognized in the Criminal Justice Act 2003. The Court of Appeal also said that the judge was not required to give the jury a special direction in relation to those parts of the confessions that incriminated the brother.

6.—VICARIOUS ADMISSIONS

31–41   In *R (on the application of Firth) v Epping Magistrates Court* [2011] EWHC 388 (Admin) a criminal defendant (and the claimant in the judicial review application) faced a charge of assault occasioning actual bodily harm. The Divisional Court held that the prosecution could respond to a defence submission during the committal hearing that the witness statements contained no evidence identifying the defendant as a person who had assaulted the victim by introducing the case management progression form in which it was stated that the only issue in the trial would be whether the defendant had acted in self-defence. The case progression form was part of the public record and, and following normal court procedures (of which the court took judicial notice), would have been completed by the defendant's agent. Toulson L.J. said (at [18]):

> "There is no reason in principle why s.118 of the Criminal Justice Act 2003 cannot apply at committal proceedings as much as it would apply at a trial. If the case progression form would be admissible in evidence at the trial there would be no rhyme or reason in excluding it from consideration at the committal stage."

Exclusion of the form would not have furthered the goal of the Criminal Procedure Rules of furthering the interests of justice, doing fairness and encouraging expedition:

> "Moreover, at the committal stage, where evidence is of possible but doubtful admissibility, it is good practice for the magistrates to admit it and leave the final decision to a higher court . . ."

At the trial, the judge can utilize s.78 of the Police and Criminal Evidence Act, 1984 to exclude the agent's admission, if admitting the evidence would be unfair to the defendant.

9.—REQUIREMENTS OF THE COMMON ENTERPRISE HEARSAY EXCEPTION

31–46   In *Bourjaily v US* 483 U.S. 171, 180 (1987) the United States Supreme Court ruled that:

". . . a co-conspirator's statements could themselves be probative of the existence of a conspiracy and the participation of both the defendant and the declarant in the conspiracy."

The Court did not, however, say that the statements were sufficient to demonstrate a conspiracy and the defendant and declarant's participation in the conspiracy without independent supporting evidence. For an example of what the prosecution has to prove in a drugs case to establish a common purpose see *R v Markovski* [2009] QCA 299.

The exception cannot apply to "statements, claims or allegations made after the common purpose has been achieved or has failed" per Lord Reed, *Johnston v H.A.* [2011] HCJAC 32 at [42]. A statement that is *contrary* to the objects of the common enterprise (such as a confession) does not fall within the common enterprise exception: *R v Heath* 2010 ONSC 3161.   **31–49**

11.—EXPERT EVIDENCE

In *R v Ahmed* [2011] EWCA Crim 184, during an application to stay proceedings for terrorism offences as an abuse of process, the judge allowed the Crown to adduce evidence from an expert engaged in the study of terrorism about the nature of Al Qaeda, its methods and organization. The expert's sources included government statements, statements from Al Qaeda, media reports, reports from organizations that specialize in the study of terrorism, and meetings with other experts in the field and people with personal knowledge of Al Qaeda. On appeal, the defence objected that the expert's evidence was inadmissible because it was based on hearsay. An analogy was drawn to Criminal Justice Act 2003, s.127, which makes provision for proof by certificate of scientific testing by someone who does not give evidence but whose tests are the basis of opinion evidence given in court. This argument was rejected. Hughes L.J. said (at [66]) that it was: **31–52**

". . . commonplace for experts to rely on hearsay material—the opinions, research and surveys of material by others are but examples. The use of such sources comes within the common law exceptions to the hearsay rule applicable to the evidence of experts, preserved by section 118 (subparagraph 8) of 2003 Act."

It is submitted that s.127 is concerned with evidence that is directly relevant to a defendant's guilt (such as the amount of alcohol in the blood, when the defendant is charged with drink-driving). The evidence about terrorism adduced in this case was background information which is why the analogy to s.127 was inappropriate.

T. Ward, "Hearsay, psychiatric evidence and the interests of justice" [2009] Crim LR 415 notes that:

". . . the wording of s.127 is wide enough to cover *any* statement made for the purposes of criminal proceedings, including for example a questionnaire completed for a psychologist assessing a defendant."

He suggests that the right response to an application to apply s.127 beyond the "preparatory work" mentioned in the cross-heading is a s.127(4) order "that it is not in the interests of justice that [the section] should apply".

CHAPTER 33

OPINION AND EXPERT EVIDENCE

4.—EXPERT OPINION

The line between opinion and factual evidence can be a fine one. Whether a statement is one or the other may be a question of degree. The distinction was considered by the Federal Court of Austria in *La Trobe Capital & Mortgage Crop v. Hay Property* [2011] FCAFC 4, (2011) 273 A.L.R. 774.

fn.43 Hodgkinson and James, *Expert Evidence, Law and Practice* 3rd edn (2010); **33–09**
Matthews and Malek, *Disclosure* 4th edn (2012), Ch.18.

5.—EXPERT EVIDENCE IN CIVIL PROCEEDINGS

(b) *System under CPR summarised*

33–22 The extent to which CPR Pt. 35 has achieved its objectives in controlling **33–22**
expert evidence and its costs is a matter of continued debate. Whilst it is clear that the
use of a joint expert is a real improvement, in other aspects it may be fairly questioned
whether expert evidence is still too readily used and at a disproportionate cost: see,
R. Jacob, 'Experts and Woolf: Have things got better?', D.Dwyer 'The role of the
expert under the CPR Pt. 33' in D. Dwyer *The Civil Procedure Rules Ten Years On*
(2010), chs 15 and 16. The cost of expert evidence remains a concern: see, Lord Justice
Jackson's *Review of Civil Litigation: Final Report* (2010), ch.38. CPR Pt. 35 and the
Practice Direction were revised in 2009.

33–23   fn.175 *The Protocol for the Instruction of Experts to give Evidence in Civil Claims* (2005) was revised in 2009.

fn.176 Various court guides have new editions, although not necessarily making changes of substance in the context of expert evidence: Chancery Guide (6th edn, 2009), paras.4.8–4.21); Admiralty and Commercial Courts Guide (9th edn, 2011), para.H2 and Appendix 11. The relevant part of the Family Proceedings Rules mirrors to a large extent CPR Pt.35: FPR, Pt.25; Practice Direction 25A—Experts and Assessors in Family Proceedings.

(ii) *Expert's duty to the Court*

33–26   CPR r.35.10 as revised now reads as follows:

"35.10

(1)   An expert's report must comply with the requirements set out in Practice Direction 35.

(2)   At the end of an expert's report there must be a statement that the expert understands and has complied with their duty to the court.

(3)   The expert's report must state the substance of all material instructions, whether written or oral, on the basis of which the report was written.

(4)   The instructions referred to in paragraph (3) shall not be privileged[(GL)] against disclosure but the court will not, in relation to those instructions –

    (a)   order disclosure of any specific document; or
    (b)   permit any questioning in court, other than by the party who instructed the expert,

unless it is satisfied that there are reasonable grounds to consider the statement of instructions given under paragraph (3) to be inaccurate or incomplete."

The numbering of the paragraphs in the Practice Direction has changed such that the general requirements for expert evidence is now found in para.2 as follows:

"Expert evidence – general requirements

2.1

Expert evidence should be the independent product of the expert uninfluenced by the pressures of litigation.

2.2

Experts should assist the court by providing objective, unbiased opinions on matters within their expertise, and should not assume the role of an advocate.

2.3

Experts should consider all material facts, including those which might detract from their opinions.

2.4

> Experts should make it clear –
> (a)   When a question or issue falls outside their expertise; and
> (b)   When they are not able to reach a definite opinion, for example because they have insufficient information.

2.5

> If, after producing a report, an expert's view changes on any material matter, such change of view should be communicated to all the parties without delay, and when appropriate to the court."

In *Medimmune Ltd v. Novartis* [2011] EWHC 1669 (Pat) at [99–114] it was stressed   **33–27** that it is the duty of the lawyers instructing the expert to ensure that any expert report is balanced and includes both the points in favour and potentially against those expressed in the report. There are various traps for the unwary which need to be avoided, otherwise the expert is liable to be vulnerable in cross examination. The lawyers need to bring home to the expert what his responsibilities are. In practice it is often the case that an expert expresses his views to the lawyer who them prepares the first draft of the report. Whilst this is permissible if properly done, there is the risk that the expert's views may become influenced by the lawyers own views on the issues.

Where an expert has already been approached by one party and given confidential   **33–29** information, it does not necessarily follow that the expert is precluded from being retained by another party. Even where the court decides to permit on expert to be called where his independence is in issue, the expert may still be cross-examined as to his independence and objectivity: *Meat Corporation of Namibia v. Dawn Meats (UK) Ltd* [2011] EWHC 474 (Ch).

fn.233 Admiralty and Commercial Courts Guide 9th edn (2011), para.H2.10;   **33–31** Chancery Guide 6th edn (2009), para.4.20 (updated citations).

(iii) *Experts' reports*

fn.241 CPR r.35.11, see further under para.33–42.   **33–32**

fn.243 CPR Pt.35 PD para.2 (revised numbering).   **33–33**
fn.244 CPR Pt.35 PD para.3.1 (revised numbering).
fn.245 CPR Pt.35 PD para.3.2(1) (revised numbering).
fn.246 CPR Pt.35 PD para.3.2(3) (revised numbering)
fn.247 CPR Pt.35 PD para.5, cross-examination as to instructions limited.
fn.249 CPR Pt.35 PD para.5 (revised numbering).
fn.252 CPR Pt.35 PD para.3.2(2) (revised numbering).
fn.253 CPR Pt.35 PD para.3.2(5) (revised numbering).
fn.254 CPR Pt.35 PD para.3.2(7) (revised numbering).
In *Dasreef v. Hawchar* [2011] HCA 21, (2011) 277 A.L.R. 611, the High Court of Australia emphasised that opinion evidence is inadmissible if the facts and assumptions on which it is based are not identified, or if those facts are not proved. The expert

should state the reasoning by which he has arrived at his conclusions based on the proven facts or assumptions.

fn.259 CPR Pt.35 PD para.3.2(6) (revised numbering).

33–34   fn.264 CPR Pt.35 PD para.6 written questions for expert (revised numbering).

fn.265 Protocol, para.16; Queen's Bench Guide, para.7.9.9; Chancery Guide 6th edn (2009), para.4.19; Admiralty and Commercial Courts Guide 9th edn (2011), para. H2.19 (written questions for expert).

fn.270 CPR Pt.35 para.3.2(9) (expert's statement as to duties).

fn.271–273 CPR Pt.35 PD para.3.3 (statement of truth).

fn.277 The authorities on whether an expert can be sued for breach of a duty of care in contract or tort by the party instructing him were extensively reviewed by the Supreme Court in *Jones v. Kaney* [2011] UKSC 13, which held that he has no immunity from such a claim.

(iv) *Court's general control of expert evidence*

33–35   CPR r.35.4 as to the Court's power to restrict expert evidence was revised in 2009 and now provides as follows:

> "35.4
>
> (1)   No party may call an expert or put in evidence an expert's report without the court's permission.
>
> (2)   When parties apply for permission they must identify –
>
>   α   the field in which expert evidence is required; and
>   β   where practicable, the name of the proposed expert.
>
>   If permission is granted it shall be in relation only to the expert named or the field identified under paragraph (2).
>
> (3A)   Where a claim has been allocated to the small claims track or the fast track, if permission is given for expert evidence, it will normally be given for evidence from only one expert on a particular issue.
>   (Paragraph 7 of Practice Direction 35 sets out some of the circumstances the court will consider when deciding whether expert evidence should be given by a single joint expert.)
>
> (4)   The court may limit the amount of a party's expert's fees and expenses that may be recovered from any other party."

33–37   fn.299 The principle that the court may grant permission to substitute an expert on condition that the previous expert's report is disclosed can even apply to a report obtained before proceedings started, but whilst the parties were acting under a pre-action protocol: *Edwards-Tubb v. J D Wetherspoon Plc* [2011] EWCA Civ 136, CA.

33–38   **The small claims track.**

fn.308 CPR, r.27.2(1)(e)—those which apply to the small claims track are CPR rr.35.1, 35.3, 35.7 and 35.9 (formerly CPR r.35.7 was also excluded).

33–39   **The fast track.**

fn.329 In both the small claims and fast tracks, CPR r.35.5(2) provides that the court will not direct an expert to attend a hearing unless it is necessary to do so in the interests of justice.

Procedure at trial.   33–42

fn.359 CPR r.35.11 provides that where a party has disclosed an expert's report, any party may use that in evidence; *Gurney Consulting Engineers v. Gleeds* [2006] EWHC 43 (TCC). CPR r.35.11 is not limited to the parties to the claim, and includes Part 20 parties: *Cooperative Group Ltd v. John Allen Associates ltd* [2010] EWHC 2300 (TCC) at [114–124]. It applies even where the party who commissioned the report has withdrawn from the proceedings: *Shepherd & Neame v. EDF Energy* [2008] EWHC 123 (TCC). Where CPR r.35.11 applies, permission of the court is not required to rely upon the expert's report, but the court nevertheless retains the power to control such evidence: *Cooperative Group Ltd v. John Allen Associates Ltd* [2010] EWHC 2300 (TCC) at [114–124]. If the expert is not called and thus his evidence not tested, this may reduce the amount of weight given to it: *Anderson v. Lyotier* [2008] EWHC 2790 (QB) at [89].

(v) *Restriction and control of expert evidence*

Limitation of the scope of disputes relating to expert evidence.   33–44

(i) *Equality of access*

fn.366 Where a request for information is made under CPR r.35.9 the information   33–45
sought must be relevant to an issue in the case: *Humber Oil Trustee Ltd v. Associated British Ports* [2011] EWHC 1184 (Ch) at [40]. See now CPR PD 35 para.4 (revised numbering).

fn.368 The relevant provisions relating to CPR r.35.6 (questions for expert) have revised citations: CPR Pt 35 PD para.6; Chancery Guide 6th edn (2009), para.4.19; Admiralty and Commercial Courts Guide 9th edn (2011), para.H2.19.

(ii) *Discussions*

fn.372 The relevant provisions relating to CPR r.35.12 (discussions between   33–46
experts) have revised citations: Admiralty and Commercial Courts Guide, 9th edn (2011), paras.H2.12–18; Chancery Guide, 6th edn (2009), paras.4.16–4.18.

(iii) *Single joint expert*   33–47

A 'single joint expert' is defined in CPR r.35.2(2) as an expert instructed to prepare a report for the court on behalf of two or more parties (including the claimant) to the proceedings. Single joint experts are the norm in cases allocated to the small claims and fast tracks: Protocol, para.17.2.

fn.389 Chancery Guide, 6th edn (2009), para.4.12 (updated citation).

fn.390 Admiralty and Commercial Courts Guide, 9th edn (2011), para.H2.2 (updated citation).

fn.393 Admiralty and Commercial Courts Guide 9th edn (2011), para. H2.3; Chancery Guide 6th edn (2009), para.4.14 (updated citations).

fn.395 It is inappropriate for a single joint expert to have discussions with one party in the absence of the other: *Childs v. Vernon & Butcher* [2007] EWCA Civ 305. Where a single joint expert has inappropriately communicated with one party's solicitor, the court may give the other party permission to rely upon another expert: *Edwards v. Bruce & Hyslop (Brucast) Ltd* [2009] EWHC 2970 (QB).

(iv) *Appointment of an assessor*

33–50   fn.403 The relevant guides relating to CPR r.35.15 and assessors have revised citations: CPR Pt 35 PD para.10; Admiralty and Commercial Courts Guide, 9th edn (2011), para.N14; Chancery Guide, 6ᵗʰ edn (2009), para.4.21.

(vi) *Acceptance of expert evidence at trial*

33–51   If a trial jungle incorrectly excludes relevant expert evidence, then on appeal a new trial may be ordered if the excluded evidence may have had an impact on the result: e.g. *Cadbury Schweppes Pty Ltd v. Darrell Lea Chocolate Shops Pty Ltd* [2007] FCAFC 70, Fed. Ct. of Australia.

6.—Expert Evidence in Criminal Proceedings

(a) *Duties of expert*

33–52   The current rules are the Criminal Procedure Rules 2011 (S.I. 2011 / 1709), Pt.33, which follow the 2010 version (as amended).

33–57   Where there has been a failure to comply with the requirements as to advance service of expert evidence in breach of Crim PR r.33.4, the courts have been prepared to exclude such evidence, particularly where it is prejudicial to another party. Thus such evidence was excluded when the defence served a report after the conclusion of the prosecution case and raised a new issue: *Writtle v. DPP* [2009] R.T.R. 28, DC. In another case the defence purported to serve a psychiatric report relating to the defendant's ability to give evidence, this was rejected as being a tactical ploy and an attempt to ambush the prosecution: *R. v. Ensor* [2009] EWCA Crim 2519, [2010] 1 Cr. App. R.18 at [32], CA. The Court of Appeal stressed the importance of raising the issue of expert evidence at the earliest practicable stage at [30]:

> "In our view the effect of CPR Parts 1.2 and 3.3 together is that it is incumbent upon both prosecution and defence parties to criminal trials to alert the court and the other side at the earliest practical moment if it is intending to adduce expert evidence. That should be done if possible at a PCMH. If it cannot be done then it must be done as soon as the possibility becomes live. The nearer the start of the trial, the greater the urgency in informing the court and the other side of the possibility of adducing expert evidence so that appropriate steps can be taken by the court and the other side to manage the expert evidence in an efficient way."

The importance of following Crim PR Pt.33 and for expert evidence to be raised at the earliest possibility was stressed by the Court of Appeal in *R v. Reed* [2009] EWCA Crim 2698, [2010] 1 Cr. App. R. 23. The Court stated at [131] that in cases involving DNA evidence:

> "
>
> i)   It is particularly important to ensure that the obligation under Rule 33.3(1) (f) and (g) is followed and also that, where propositions are to be advanced as part of an evaluative opinion (of the type given by Valerie Tomlinson

in the present case), that each proposition is spelt out with precision in the expert report.

ii)   Expert reports must, after each has been served, be carefully analysed by the parties. Where a disagreement is identified, this must be brought to the attention of the court.

iii)   If the reports are available before the PCMH, this should be done at the PCMH; but if the reports have not been served by all parties at the time of the PCMH (as may often be the case), it is the duty of the Crown and the defence to ensure that the necessary steps are taken to bring the matter back before the judge where a disagreement is identified.

iv)   It will then in the ordinary case be necessary for the judge to exercise his powers under Rule 33.6 and make an order for the provision of a statement.

v)   We would anticipate, even in such a case, that, as was eventually the position in the present appeal, much of the science relating to DNA will be common ground. The experts should be able to set out in the statement under Rule 33.6 in clear terms for use at the trial the basic science that is agreed, in so far as it is not contained in one of the reports. The experts must then identify with precision what is in dispute—for example, the match probability, the interpretation of the electrophoretograms or the evaluative opinion that is to be given.

vi)   If the order as to the provisions of the statement under Rule 33.6 is not observed and in the absence of a good reason, then the trial judge should consider carefully whether to exercise the power to refuse permission to the party whose expert is in default to call that expert to give evidence. In many cases, the judge may well exercise that power. A failure to find time for a meeting because of commitments to other matters, a common problem with many experts as was evident in this appeal, is not to be treated as a good reason."

In *R v. Henderson* [2010] 2 Cr. App. R.24, [2010] EWCA Crim 1269 at [200–220], the Court of Appeal stressed the importance of proper case management in cases of conflicting medical evidence which may have an important part in the case.

7.—EXPERT EVIDENCE AS TO COMPETENCY AND CREDIT

For a review of the case law as to admissibility, see Law Commission Consultation   **33–62**
Paper, *Admissibility of Expert Evidence in Criminal Proceedings in England and Wales* (2009).

So long as the expert evidence falls within the two-fold test in *Bonython* (1984) 38 S.A.S.R. 45, the existence of a possible conflict of interest (such as a prior relationship between the expert and the party calling him) does not automatically disqualify the expert from giving evidence, albeit it may go to weight as opposed to admissibility: *R. v. Stubbs* [2006] EWCA Crim 2312; *Leo Sawrijj Ltd v. North Cumbria Magistrates' Court* [2009] EWHC 2823 (Admin), [2010] 1 Cr. App. R. 22.

In *R. v. Reed* [2009] EWCA Crim 2698, [2010] 1 Cr. App. R. 23 at [111] the Court of Appeal confirmed the principles as to the admissibility of expert evidence. First, expert evidence of a scientific nature is not admissible where the scientific basis on which it is based is not sufficiently reliable for it to be put before a jury. There is no enhanced test of admissibility for such evidence. Secondly, even if the scientific basis is sufficiently reliable, the evidence is not admissible unless it is within the scope of evidence an expert can properly give. Thirdly, unless the admissibility is challenged, the judge will admit that evidence. If objection is taken, then it is for the party proffering the evidence to prove its admissibility.

9.—VALUE OF EXPERT EVIDENCE

33–66   In *R.v. Khan (Dawood)* [2009] EWCA Crim 1569, [2010] 1 Cr. App. R.4, the uncontested expert evidence was that the defendant to a charge of murder was suffering from an abnormality of mind induced by disease. There was also uncontradicted evidence that if the defendant had killed the victim that abnormality would have substantially affected his mental responsibility for his actions. The judge refused to withdraw the charge of murder and the jury convicted. The Court of Appeal upheld the judge's approach. The court observed that there is no simple scientific test of whether a defendant's mental responsibility for his acts or omissions in doing a killing was substantially impaired. It was a question for the jury to decide on the basis of the medical and factual evidence. *Walton v. R* [1978] AC 788, PC and *R. v. Byrne* [1960] 2 Q.B. 396, CA were applied.

In *R v Hookway* [2011] EWCA Crim 1989, the court held that it was open to the jury to consider the conflicting evidence, eg. the two expert witnesses, and place whatever weight they considered appropriate on the opinion of either expert, hence the court rejected the contention that the DNA evidence should have been withdrawn from the jury. The case was difference from *Cannings*, because inter alia, the prosecution case did not depend exclusively, or almost exclusively, on the prosecution DNA evidence, and the dispute between the experts was not whether there was any DNA evidence incriminating the defendants, but the strength of that evidence.

10.—SUBJECTS OF EXPERT EVIDENCE

(f) *Foreign law*

33–75   Expert opinion evidence as to the proper application of the foreign law to the specific facts of the case was held to be an inadmissible intrusion into the judicial function as to the ultimate issue: *Noza Holdings Pty Ltd v. Commissioner of Taxation* [2010] FCA 990, (2011) 273 A.L.R. 621, Fed. Ct. of Australia.

(i) *Facts*

33–79   It is permissible to adduce expert evidence to establish historical facts: *R. v. Sawoniuk* [2002] 2 Cr. App. R. 220, CA (Nazi policy towards the Jews); *R. v. Ahmed and Ahmed* [2011] EWCA Crim 184, CA. (Al Qaeda as a terrorist organisation); *Berezovsky v. Hine* [2011] EWHC 1176 (Ch) (contemporary Russian history).

(j) *Identity*

33–80   For the admissibility of expert evidence in relation to Low Template DNA, see *R. v. Reed* [2009] EWCA Crim 2698, [2010] 1 Cr. App. R. 23, CA; A. Jamieson, 'LCN DNA analysis and opinion on transfer: *R. v. Reed and Reed*', (2011) 15 E&P 161–169; M. Naughton and G. Tan, 'The need for caution in the use of DNA evidence to avoid convicting the innocent', (2011) 15 E&P 245–257.

In *R. v. Otway* [2011] EWCA Crim 3, evidence from a podiatrist as to the gait of a person identified in CCTV evidence was held to have been correctly admitted.

Footwear mark expert evidence was considered in detail by the Court of Appeal in *R. v. T* [2010] EWCA Crim 2439,[2011] 1 Cr. App. R.9, where the main issue was whether the expert should provide a quantitative analysis for the likelihood of the shoes in question having made the marks (see further under Ch.34 below). See also M. Redmayne et al 'Forensic Science Evidence in Question' [2011] Crim. L.R. 347.

Fingerprint expert evidence was reviewed by the Court of Appeal in *R v. Smith (Peter)* [2011] EWCA Crim 1296, [2011] 2 Cr. App. R.16, which expressed concern as to the practices and standards applied in that area.

fn.627a *R. v. Atkins and Atkins* [2009] EWCA Crim 1876, [2010] 1 Cr. App. R.8—expert evidence from facial mapping expert as to identity of person identified in CCTV evidence (updated citation); G. Edmond et al. '*Atkins v. The Emperor*: the 'cautious' use of unreliable 'expert' opinion', (2010) 14 E&P 146–166.

(k) *Mental state*

In the context of a defendant's fitness to plead, save in clear cases, a court must **33–81** rigorously examine evidence of psychiatrists before concluding a defendant is unfit to plead. The fact that psychiatrists agree is not enough, save in clear cases. A court would be failing in its duty to the public and a defendant if it did not rigorously examine the evidence and reach its own conclusion: *R v. Walls* [2011] EWCA Crim 443, [2011] 2 Cr. App. R.6 at [38].

STATISTICAL AND SURVEY EVIDENCE

2.—CLASSICAL STATISTICS

(b) *Drawing inferences*

(i) *Reference classes and base rates*

In *R v T*,[1] the Court of Appeal considered expert evidence on the likelihood that **34–10** it was the appellant's trainers, rather than anyone else's, that had made marks found at a crime scene. The case highlights the importance of identifying the correct reference class, against which a sample should be compared.[2] It was possible to compare the defendant's shoe against either a database held by the Forensic Science Service, which was made up of what came into FSS laboratories, or a database consisting of frequencies of distribution of all shoes by manufacturers. In the former, the shoe pattern in question was relatively frequent (i.e. the database is representative of the sort of shoes worn by people commonly associated with crime scenes), while in the latter, the mark was relatively infrequent (i.e. the database is representative of the population as a whole, most of whom are not associated with crime scenes). The choice of reference class therefore significantly affected the calculation of the likelihood.[3]

---

[1] *R v T* [2010] EWCA Crim 2439, [2011] 1 Cr App 85.
[2] [2010] EWCA Crim 2439, at [42]–[43].
[3] The Bayesian likelihood ratio was derived from the probability that the marks discovered at the scene would have been observed if the trainers owned by the appellant had made the marks, divided by the probability that the marks would have been observed if those trainers had not made the marks. See para.[34–38], below.

4.—Bayesian Statistics

(a) *Bayes' Theorem*

34–36   At the heart of the Bayesian approach is what is called the "likelihood ratio". This measures the probative force of a piece of evidence relative to two hypotheses: in a legal context usually the probability of the evidence given the prosecution hypothesis (represented as "$P(E|H_p)$"), divided by the probability of the evidence given the defence hypothesis ("$P(E|H_D)$").[4] The likelihood ratio is then adjusted by adding in the background information available ("I"):

$$\frac{P(E|H_p, I)}{P(E|H_D, I)}$$

Finally, the likelihood ratio for a piece of evidence is combined with what are known as the "prior odds", in order to produce the "posterior odds". The prior odds represent the probability that a hypothesis was the case before this particular piece of evidence is considered. The posterior odds are the probability of real interest to the court.

$$\underset{\text{posterior odds}}{\frac{P(H_p|E, I)}{P(H_D|E, I)}} = \underset{\text{likelihood ratio}}{\frac{P(E|H_p, I)}{P(E|H_D, I)}} \times \underset{\text{prior odds}}{\frac{P(H_p|I)}{P(H_D|I)}}$$

(b) *The view of the courts*

34–38   In *R v T*,[5] the Court of Appeal again considered the use of Bayesian statistics as evidence in criminal trials.[6] The Court considered the use of likelihood ratios in the provision of an evaluative opinion where the statistical data available were uncertain or incomplete. The issue at trial had been whether a footwear mark found at a crime scene had been made by the defendant. The prosecution brought expert evidence on footwear matching, using a Bayesian approach.

The Court of Appeal rejected the use of the Bayesian approach on the basis that mathematical formulae should only be considered only where there is firm, reliable statistical data, as is available with DNA expert evidence "and possibly other areas".[7] From a statistical perspective, this view is not strictly correct, since the Bayesian

---

[4] M. Redmayne, *Expert Evidence and Criminal Justice* (Oxford University Press, 2001), Ch.3.
[5] *R v T* [2010] EWCA Crim 2439, [2011] 1 Cr App 85.
[6] The previous appellate consideration being *R. v Adams* (No. 1) [1996] 2 Cr.App.R. 467 CA; *R. v Adams* (No. 2) [1998] 1 Cr. App.R. 377. Although it is generally considered by lawyers that the second Court of Appeal in *Adams* firmly rejected the use of Bayesianism, it has recently been suggested that this is wrong, as the use of Bayesian statistics was not in fact argued before that court: B. Robertson, G. A. Vignaux and C. Berger, "Extending the Confusion about Bayes" (2011) 74(3) MLR 444–455, 451.
[7] [2010] EWCA Crim 2439, at [77]–[80], [90].

formulae are matters of logic rather than mathematics: they propose a way in which pieces of information should be combined to make a valid inference. As such, the values used in Bayesian calculations need not represent "hard data".

Where an expert lacks a reliable data source, it remains open for him to present a subjective opinion in a report, making it clear that this opinion is based on his experience. Any expert report should be transparent as to the method by which the expert arrived at his opinion. The word "scientific" should not be used in this context, however, as it may give the jury an impression of precision and objectivity that is not present.[8]

A Bayesian likelihood ratio approach, relating to firearm discharge residue, was also taken in *R v George*.[9] It seems likely, in light of the approach of the Court of Appeal in *R v T*, that if the Court of Appeal in *George* had directly considered the merits of the likelihood ratio approach, rather than simply taking it as part of its consideration of the overall evidence, then that approach, and the associated firearm discharge residue evidence, might have been considered unfavourably.[10]

The Court in *R v T* declined to decide how likelihood ratios should be used in expert footwear mark evidence and how the use of likelihood ratios should be explained to a jury.[11]

5.—SURVEY EVIDENCE

(b) *Survey methodology*

One of the main reasons that parties are required to seek permission to carry out 34–42 a survey is so that consideration can be given to the probative value and cost of the evidence before the bulk of the money is spent. That objective may be defeated if the opposing party saves its criticisms for trial, since then it is too late to modify the survey in response. That said, a failure to express criticisms at the application stage may be "unhelpful", but it does not necessarily estop a party from subsequently raising criticisms at trial, at least in those circumstances where the party has indicated that it does not think that a survey would serve a useful purpose.[12]

(c) *The value of survey evidence*

There is a distinction between a simple witness gathering exercise and a survey 34–44 which is designed and conducted in such a way as to be able to attach statistical significance to the results, and so to extrapolate to the wider population. A witness identified as the result of a witness gathering exercise may nevertheless be referred to as a 'survey witness', to distinguish them from other types of witness, but they are not be seen as statistically representative of a wider population.[13]

---

[8] [2010] EWCA Crim 2439, at [96].
[9] *R v Barry George* [2007] EWCA Crim 2722.
[10] [2010] EWCA Crim 2439, at [90].
[11] [2010] EWCA Crim 2439, at [88].
[12] *Diageo North America Inc & Anor v Intercontinental Brands (ICB) Ltd and Ors* [2010] EWHC 17 (Ch), [161].
[13] *Whirlpool Corporation and Ors v Kenwood Ltd* [2009] EWCA Civ 753, [15], [25].

RESTRICTIONS ON THE RIGHT TO SILENCE

3.—PRE-TRIAL SILENCE

(a) *Reliance upon a fact*

35–08 fn.48 See also *R v Chivers* [2011] EWCA Crim 1212 at [45], where no inference could be drawn from the fact that the defendant said something for the first time at trial which was accepted by both sides as true.

fn.50 Cf. *R. v Davis* [2010] EWCA Crim 708 in which the trial judge correctly gave a s.34 direction in a case where the appellant did not dispute the accuracy of what surveillance officer said he had been doing, but claimed all his activities had an innocent explanation.

(c) *The role of legal advice*

35–11 fn.74 In *R. v Smith* (Troy Nicholas) [2011] EWCA Crim 1098 the defendant gave evidence at his trial that he had given a "no comment" interview on legal advice, and the trial judge gave a s.34 direction without first hearing submissions from counsel as to whether it was appropriate. As the facts identified could not properly give rise to an inference of guilt, his conviction was quashed on appeal.

35–12 *R. v Parradine* [2011] EWCA Crim 656 is another case following *R. v Knight* [2004] 1 Cr App R 9 and *R. v Turner* [2004] 1 All ER 1025 in which a s.34 direction was correctly given because the defendant in his prepared written statement to the police had failed to mention details which he subsequently gave evidence about at his trial.

R. v Seaton [2010] EWCA Crim 1980; [2011] 1 WLR 623 provides a useful guide to the law relating to waiver of legal professional privilege by a defendant seeking to avoid an adverse inference being drawn under s.34. The defendant was charged with murder, and in his two prepared statements he gave different explanations as to how he had cut his hand, a significant issue given that the victim had been stabbed to death with a variety of weapons. The defendant gave evidence that the first statement he had signed contained an erroneous account of how he came to be injured, and in cross-examination attributed this mistake to his solicitor who had prepared the document, and said that after a discussion with her he had decided not to change the statement. The trial judge ruled that counsel for the Crown was entitled to comment to the jury on the absence of the solicitor from the witness box to rebut its submission that his account was recent fabrication which had been fashioned to take account of the evidence as it emerged. The Court of Appeal ruled that this comment was proper as he had partially waived legal professional privilege, and explained *R v Wilmot* (1989) 89 Cr App Rep 341 as authority only for the proposition that a defendant who volunteered evidence of his communications with his solicitor did not breach privilege; the privilege was his to waive. Its analysis of four subsequent cases concerned with s.34: *R. v Condron and Condron* [1997] 1 WLR 827, [1997] 1 Cr App Rep 185; *R. v Bowden* [1999] 4 All ER 43, [1999] 2 Cr App Rep 176; *R. v Wishart* [2005] EWCA Crim 1337 and *R v Loizou* [2006] EWCA Crim 1719 led it to conclude at [43]:

"

a) Legal professional privilege is of paramount importance. There is no question of balancing privilege against other considerations of public interest: *R v Derby Justices ex parte B.*

b) Therefore, in the absence of waiver, no question can be asked which intrudes upon privilege. That means, inter alia, that if a suggestion of recent fabrication is being pursued at trial, a witness, including the Defendant, cannot, unless he has waived privilege, be asked whether he told his counsel or solicitor what he now says is the truth. Such a question would require him either to waive his privilege or suffer criticism for not doing so. If any such question is asked by an opposing party (whether the Crown or a co-accused) the judge must stop it, tell the witness directly that he does not need to answer it, and explain to the jury that no one can be asked about things which pass confidentially between him and his lawyer. For the same reasons, in the absence of waiver, the witness cannot be asked whether he is willing to waive.

c) However, the Defendant is perfectly entitled to open up his communication with his lawyer, and it may sometimes be in his interest to do so. One example of when he may wish to do so is to rebut a suggestion of recent fabrication. Another may be to adduce in evidence the reasons he was advised not to answer questions. If he does so, there is no question of breach of privilege, because he cannot be in breach of his own privilege. What is happening is that he is waiving privilege.

d) If the Defendant does give evidence of what passed between him and his solicitor he is not thereby waiving privilege entirely and generally, that is to say he does not automatically make available to all other parties everything that he said to his solicitor, or his solicitor to him, on every occasion. He may well not even be opening up everything said on the occasion of which he gives evidence, and not on topics unrelated to that of which he gives evidence. The test is fairness and/or the avoidance of a misleading impression. It is that the Defendant should not, as it has been put in some of the cases, be able both to "have his cake and eat it".

e) If a Defendant says that he gave his solicitor the account now offered at trial, that will ordinarily mean that he can be cross examined about exactly what he told the solicitor on that topic, and if the comment is fair another party can comment upon the fact that the solicitor has not been called to confirm something which, if it is true, he easily could confirm. If it is intended to pursue cross examination beyond what is evidently opened up, the proper extent of it can be discussed and the judge invited to rule.

f)   A Defendant who adduces evidence that he was advised by his lawyer not to answer questions but goes no further than that does not thereby waive privilege. This is the ratio of *Bowden* and is well established. After all, the mere fact of the advice can equally well be made evident by the solicitor announcing at the interview that he gives it then and there, and there is then no revelation whatever of any private conversation between him and the Defendant.

g)   But a Defendant who adduces evidence of the content of, or reasons for, such advice, beyond the mere fact of it, does waive privilege at least to the extent of opening up questions which properly go to whether such reason can be the true explanation for his silence: Bowden. That will ordinarily include questions relating to recent fabrication, and thus to what he told his solicitor of the facts now relied upon at trial: *Bowden* and *Loizou*.

h)   The rules as to privilege and waiver, and thus as to cross examination and comment, are the same whether it is the Crown or a co-accused who challenges the Defendant."

fn.102 See *R v Hackett* [2011] EWCA Crim 380 at [25]–[29] and *R. v Gelardo* [2011]   **35–14**
EWCA Crim 1901 at [28]. In the latter case, the defendant, who had made several statements to the police, had said in evidence that he had asked for an interview to be suspended to enable him to speak with his solicitor—that he had told his solicitor that he wanted to change his story—but that his solicitor had advised him not to do so. This prompted the trial judge to ask what risk there could have been in changing his account in order to tell the truth, but this intervention simply "voice a thought that was bound to go through the jury's minds", and a s.34 direction was appropriate even though it had not been argued that the appellant had been trying to hide behind his solicitor's advice.

It was conceded in *Adetoro v United Kingdom* [2010] ECHR 46834/06 that the trial judge had given a flawed s.34 direction, having failed to direct the jury that adverse inferences may only be drawn where the jury is satisfied that the real reason for the defendant's silence is that he has no answer to the questions asked, or no answer that would hold up to scrutiny. Although the direction did not comply with domestic law, it did not render the conviction unsafe. At [51] the European Court of Human Rights described two explanations for a defendant's silence:

"The Court further observes that an accused may choose to remain silent during police interviews for a number of reasons. Some will be unconnected with the accused's substantive defence. Such cases include where the accused has remained silent on the advice of his lawyer or because he does not consider that he is sufficiently lucid to understand the questions asked or the nature of the proceedings (see, for example, *Beckles* and *Condron*, both cited above). In other cases, an accused will choose not to answer questions at a police interview for a reason which is inherently linked to his substantive defence. Such cases generally arise where the accused has some reason to conceal the truth. In such cases, it is artificial to separate consideration of the substantive defence from consideration of the explanation for the accused's silence because in order to accept the plausibility of the explanation for the applicant's silence, the plausibility of the applicant's account of events from which the reason for silence stems must also be accepted."

The instant case fell into the latter category because the defendant's explanation for remaining silent was essentially the same as his defence, namely that he was involved in a conspiracy to buy and sell stolen cars (rather than a conspiracy to rob), and had remained silent in order to avoid incriminating other people involved with the stolen vehicles. It could be concluded from the fact that the jury rejected his defence that it also rejected his explanation for his silence.

R. v Martin [2011] EWCA Crim 868 raised a novel issue as to the interpretation and effect of s.34 of the Criminal Justice and Public Order Act 1994. The defendant was interviewed by the police on December 17 who were under the impression that the complainant had alleged that she had been raped by him on December 15 rather in September. He gave a no comment interview and then his solicitor read out a prepared statement denying that he had raped the complainant at his house on December 15. At his trial for committing rape on September 6, a s.34 direction was given because the defendant relied upon a number of matters which he had failed to mention when he was interviewed, including his very limited knowledge of the complainant, his total absence of any general sexual contact with her, his very limited communication with her in view of her disability, and the return of his partner to the house shortly after the time when this incident allegedly occurred. The Court of Appeal quashed his

conviction. It held that it was immaterial to the application of s.34(1)(a) that the date of the rape put to the appellant was not the date alleged in the indictment, since that was not an essential part of the charge. However, it was necessary to consider whether a jury could reasonably conclude that there was any "fact which in the circumstances existing at the time the accused could reasonably have been expected to mention when . . . questioned". In his prepared statement that he had denied committing rape on December 15, and it was common ground at trial that this denial was truthful. It is difficult to see how in those circumstances he could have been reasonably expected to say more. Moreover, given the nature of his defence, he could not be said to have failed to mention any fact that could reasonably give rise to an adverse inference. Some of the facts were accepted as true, such as his limited communication with her, others were little more than a denial of the offence, and he could not reasonably have been expected to mention anything relating to any incident in September when he was being interviewed about an alleged incident that occurred two days earlier.

6.—Scope of Section 35

35–19   fn.27 It was unsuccessfully argued that it would be undesirable for the defendant to give evidence because the condition of his mental health in *R. v Tabbakh* [2009] EWCA Crim 464; *R. v Charisma* [2009] EWCA Crim 2345 and *R. v Barry* [2010] EWCA Crim 195; [2010] 1 Cr. App. R. 32.

7.—"Proper" Inferences of Guilt

35–20   fn.136 In *R. v Clark* [2010] EWCA Crim 1181 the trial judge mistakenly received the impression that the defendant had been advised by counsel that the stage had been reached when he could give evidence if he so wished, and that he had been advised of the consequences of not doing so. The procedure by which the trial judge satisfied himself about those matters did not comply with s.35(2), and therefore an adverse inference direction under s.35 should not have been given. In *R. v Hamidi*

[2010] EWCA Crim 66 a co-accused had absconded before the necessary statutory procedure for a s.35 direction had been satisfied, but this did not render unfair the direction concerning the two appellants who refused to testify. This may have given the absentee an advantage he did not deserve, but this was not correspondingly unfair to the co-appellants since they had made an informed decision not to give evidence.

CHAPTER 36

CONFESSIONS

5.—ADMISSIBILITY UNDER THE POLICE AND CRIMINAL EVIDENCE ACT 1984 SECTION 76

On the meaning of "oppression" under s.76(2)(a) of the Police and Criminal Evidence Act 184 see *R. v Dhorajiwala* [2010] EWCA Crim 1237; [2010] 2 Cr. App. R. 21 at [26] and *R v. JA* [2010] EWCA Crim 1506 at [24]–[25]. **36–06**

fn. 64 In *Richardson v Chief Constable of West Midlands* [2011] EWHC 773 (QB) there no reasonable basis for arresting under PACE s.24(4) a suspect who was **36–09** voluntarily attending police station for interview and he was awarded damages for false imprisonment.

Revised versions of PACE Codes A (Stop and Search), B (Searching Premises) and D(Identification) came into force in March 2011 by virtue of SI 2011 No 412. The full text of all the PACE Codes is available from http://www.homeoffice.gov.uk/police/powers/pace-codes/

7.—DISCRETIONARY EXCLUSION OF CONFESSIONS

36–11   *R. v* Scott [2010] EWCA Crim 3212 is an unusual case where the accused made a nine minute emergency call shortly after allegedly shooting the victim with a cross-bow. The Court of Appeal, in upholding the decision to admit the contents of the call, appears to have taken a strict view of what amounts to a confession. It also held that law relating to those formally interviewed at police stations were inapplicable to such a conversation, and took a strict view of whether the accused was mentally handicapped for the purposes of s.77 of the Police and Criminal Evidence Act.

36–12   In *Cadder v HM Advocate* [2010] UK SC 43; [2010] 1 WLR 2601 the Supreme Court applied the decision of the European Court of Human Rights in *Salduz v Turkey* (2008) 49 EHRR 42, and, overturning *HM Advocate v McLean* [200] HCJAC 97, decided that s.14 of the Criminal Procedure (Scotland) Act 1995 which permitted a detainee to be questioned without access to legal advice did not comply with Art. 6. This provision was swiftly amended by the Criminal Procedure (Legal Assistance, Detention and Appeals) (Scotland) Act 2010.

January 2011 marked the 25th anniversary of the right to legal advice conferred by s.58 of the Police and Criminal Evidence Act1984. For recent empirical research into the impact of this right see Pattenden and Skinns [2010] 73 Mod LR 349 and Pleasence, Kemp and Balmer [2011] Crim LR.

fn.114 *Cf R v. JA* [2010] EWCA Crim 1506 in which it was held that the police had not deliberately lied to the appellant. Even if there had been an innocent misrepresentation, it was not likely to render any confession unreliable, or justify the exercise of the s.78 discretion. See also *Charles v. DPP* [2009] EWHC 3521 (Admin); [2010] RTR 34, QB where the defendant, having been informed that he would be charged with being in charge of a motor vehicle whilst unfit through drink, was asked half way through the interview whether he had been driving his car, without being warned by the police that they were now investigating a more serious offence. His voluntary admission was excluded under s.78 because of two serious breaches of Code C in relation to the cautions he received which undermined important protections accorded to detainees under PACE.

36–13   fn.136 *R. v M* [2011] EWCA Crim 648 followed *R. v Looseley, A-G's Reference (No.3 of 2000)* and it was not open for the trial judge to make a finding of entrapment where an undercover police officer had insinuated himself into the defendant's confidence and done no more than offer him the opportunity to commit a criminal offence.

36–14   While the courts state that they have a broad discretion to stay proceedings for abuse of process where evidence has been obtained improperly, the decision of the Privy Council in *Warren v. AG for Jersey* [2011] UKPC 10; [2011] 3 WLR 464 demonstrates that the public interest in ensuring that those accused of serious crimes are convicted tends to outweigh executive misconduct. The only evidence against the accused, charged with conspiracy to import a large quantity of drugs, was derived from an unlawful audio device and the misconduct of the Jersey police involved misleading the Attorney General, the Chief Police Officer of Jersey and the authorities of three foreign states. Public authorities tempted to flout the law may not be deterred by Lord Hope's warning at [63]:

> "It was a sustained, deliberate and, one might say, cynical act of law-breaking . . . But the result of this appeal must not be taken as an indication that conduct of this kind will always lead to the same conclusion."

9.—PROCEDURE: THE CROWN COURT

If the trial Judge wrongly determines that there is no viable grounds for exclusion under s 76 and fails to hold a voir dire under s.76(3), the consequence is that the Crown has failed to prove beyond reasonable doubt that the confession did not fall foul of s.76(2)(a) or (b), and the confession must be excluded: *R. v Dhorajiwala* [2010] EWCA Crim 1237; [2010] 2 Cr. App. R. 21.   **36–16**

21.—LIES OF THE ACCUSED

fn.281 A good example of an inappropriate and erroneous *Lucas* direction can be found in *R. v W* [2010] EWCA Crim 307. It was not clear that the appellant had told a lie, and moreover the *Lucas* direction, using the word "lie" or "liar" eight times gave undue prominence to the issue.   **36–37**

In *R. v Hackett* [2011] EWCA Crim 380; [2011] 2 Cr.App.R. 35 the Court of Appeal endorsed the principle laid down in *R. v Rana* [2007] EWCA Crim 2261, that it was usually unhelpful and confusing to give a jury both a s.34 direction and a *Lucas* direction; the trial judge should select and adapt whichever seems more appropriate on the facts of the case. Where both directions are given, it is important that the directions are consistent, a point emphasised in *R. v Stanislas* [2004] EWCA Crim 226.

CHAPTER 37

STATEMENTS IN THE PRESENCE, AND DOCUMENTS IN THE POSSESSION OF A PARTY

1.—PRINCIPLE

(b) *Statements in absence*

Thakrar v R. [2010] EWCA Crim 1505 concerns the admissibility of confessional **37–03** evidence under the hearsay provisions of the Criminal Justice Act 2003 ss.114, 116 and 121, rather than s.76 of the Police and Criminal Evidence Act 1984 . The evidence took the form of formal written statements provided by three identifiable witnesses interviewed by the police in Northern Cyprus, who were not willing to come to the UK to testify at the joint trial of two brothers for a series of brutal murders (satisfying s.116(2)). The written statements referred to boasts allegedly made by Miran Thakrar which revealed a detailed knowledge of the crimes and therefore amounted to confessions, and which also incriminated his brother Kevan as an accomplice. The trial judge concluded that it was not feasible to edit the statements so as to conceal the identity of Miran's accomplice. The reliability and probative value of this double hearsay evidence was high and it was admitted against Miran in the interests of justice under s.121(1)(c). The Court of Appeal described the trial judge's approach to the admission of the statements against Miran as impeccable and also upheld the use of the hearsay as evidence against Kevan. There was no justification for excluding those parts of the confession which incriminated him, given its reliability and value in relation to his defence of alibi. There were no grounds for trying Kevan separately, and in any case the Court of Appeal did not accept counsel's contention that in such circumstances the evidence of Miran's confession would not have been admitted against him. Kevan had not been present when the assertions that he had committed a crime were made, and therefore had not adopted them. Miran's confession could not have been used against him at common law (See para.36–29). The admissibility of such evidence via the 2003 Act has been touched on in several cases (See para.36–28 footnote 233), but *Thakrar* is the first to decide (albeit in the course of one paragraph) that such hearsay was admissible evidence. No reference was made to s.128(2), which provides that nothing in the hearsay provisions of the 2003 Act makes a confession admissible if it would not be admissible under ss.76 and 76A of the Police and Criminal Evidence Act.

CHAPTER 38

AGENCY, PARTNERSHIP, COMPANIES, COMMON PURPOSE, ACTING IN A CAPACITY

1.—AGENCY

(b) *Criminal cases*

The Criminal Justice Act 2003 s.118(1)(6)(a) preserves the common law rule that an **38–04** admission by an agent of a defendant is admissible against the defendant as evidence of any matter stated. Toulson LJ in R. (Firth) v Epping Magistrates' Court [2011] EWHC 388 (Admin) stated at [18]:

> "There is no reason in principle why section 118 of the Criminal Justice Act 2003 cannot apply at committal proceedings as much as it would apply at a trial. If the case progression form would be admissible in evidence at the trial there would be no rhyme or reason in excluding it from consideration at the committal stage. Moreover, at the committal stage, where evidence is of possible but doubtful admissibility, it is good practice for the magistrates to admit it and leave the final decision to a higher court, as the magistrates correctly did in the present case."

3.—CORPORATIONS

The Bribery Act 2010 c.23 is now in force and of particular note is s.7, which creates **38–10** an offence of failing to prevent bribery, which can be committed only by a "relevant commercial organisation". This is defined in s.7(5) as a body incorporated under the law of any part of the United Kingdom and which carries on business whether there or elsewhere, a partnership that is formed under the law of any part of the United Kingdom and which carries on business there or elsewhere, or any other body corporate or partnership wherever incorporated or formed which carries on business in any part of the United Kingdom. The corporate offences are discussed by Gentle in [2011] Crim L.R. 101.

4.—ACTS AND DECLARATIONS IN PURSUANCE OF A COMMON PURPOSE

38–13   The common enterprise exception to the hearsay rule was discussed in *R v Sofroniou* [2009] EWCA Crim 1360 at [44]–[49], with particular reference to whether a statement was a narration of past events and so outside the scope of the exception, or a running record of the ongoing conspiracy.

CHAPTER 39

JUDICIAL DISCRETION TO ADMIT OR EXCLUDE EVIDENCE

2.—R. v SANG

R. v Sang has since been applied, considered or referred to in over a hundred reported cases.   **39–04**

4.—POLICE AND CRIMINAL EVIDENCE ACT 1984 SECTION 78

For further discussion (see n.41) of s.78, *R. v Sang* and entrapment, see "Beyond the   **39–10**
Judicial Pale" (2009) 27 I.L.T. 289 by David Brooke.

9.—EUROPEAN CONVENTION ON HUMAN RIGHTS

R. v Ibrahim and others [2008] EWCA Crim 880; [2009] 1 W.L.R. 578 arose out   **39–21**
of the failed terrorist attacks in London on July 21, 2005. Pursuant to Sch.8 para.8
of the Terrorism Act 2000, a senior police officer had authorised a delay in permitting the defendants to consult solicitors. In the course of their "safety" interviews,
the defendants made a number of untrue assertions undermining their defences at
trial. They submitted that this evidence should be excluded under s.78 of the Police
and Criminal Evidence Act 1984 and that to admit it would breach their article 6
Convention rights. That submission was rejected, the evidence was admitted and the
defendants were convicted. The Court of Appeal, considering also section 34(2A) of

the Criminal Justice and Public Order Act 1984 (adverse inferences: see para.35–13 of the 17th edition of this work at page 1193), held that the question whether the "safety" interviews evidence should be used in evidence at trial was subject to the ordinary principles governing fair trials and the overarching provisions in s.78. Admission of evidence in cases such as these turns in particular on the nature of the warning or caution, if any, given by the police ahead of the "safety" interview, whether the evidence obtained was directly relevant to the charge or whether the first connection established by the prosecution against the defendant in question with respect to the offence arose out of the interview. Leave to appeal against conviction was refused.

In *R. v K(A)* [2009] EWCA Crim 1640; [2010] 2 W.L.R. 905, the trial judge ruled that certain admissions made by the defendant in earlier ancillary relief proceedings post-divorce were admissible at his trial for cheating the public revenue. The Court of Appeal (considering *Saunders v United Kingdom* (1996) 23 E.H.R.R. 313) allowed the defendant's appeal. It held that the use of the admissions in the ancillary relief proceedings would deprive the defendant of the fair trial to which he was entitled under article 6 of the Convention and had therefore to be excluded under s.78.

10.—Other Aspects of Section 78

(a) *The effect on co-defendants*

39–22   In *R. v Downer* [2009] EWCA Crim 1361; [2010] 1 W.L.R. 846, the trial judge ruled that the co-defendants' guilty pleas should not be excluded under s.78 and in summing up the case to the jury he stated that the co-defendants had pleaded guilty to the very offence with which the defendant stood charged (for which he was subsequently convicted). The Court of Appeal, allowing the defendant's appeal, held that the admission of the pleas was so prejudicial it should have been excluded under s.78 and that the judge's error was exacerbated by his summing up.

39–26   Up-to-date Codes are available on the Home Office website, www.homeoffice.gov.uk (accessed August 30, 2011).

(e) *Breaches of the Police and Criminal Evidence Act 1984 and the Codes of Practice*

In *R. (Cook) v Serious Organised Crime Agency* [2010] EWHC 2119 (Admin); [2011] 1 W.L.R. 144, DC, the agency had conceded that the execution of warrants and the seizure of material had been unlawful. The claimant had been permitted to take documents away from a police station, but the agency then purported to re-seize them. The claim for judicial review was upheld, but the Court refused to order destruction of the documents or prohibit the use of the knowledge or information contained in them. Its rationale was that material unlawfully obtained could be admitted in evidence, applying *R. v Sang* [1980] A.C. 402, subject to control under s.78.

(g) *Identification evidence*

39–28   *Attorney General's Reference (No.2 of 2002)* [2002] EWCA Crim 2373; [2003] 1 Crim.App.R. 321 considered (amongst others) in *R. v Moss* [2011] EWCA Crim 252;

[2011] Crim. L.R. 560. In the latter case, the prosecution relied upon the evidence of an off-duty police officer who had gone to the police station to check his emails in the course of which he passed a colleague's computer screen, saw a CCTV image from the burglary in issue and said, "That's Alvin Moss" (the defendant). The trial judge declined to exclude this identification evidence under s.78 of the Police and Criminal Evidence Act 1984. The Court of Appeal dismissed the appeal against conviction, not least because the trial judge had given the jury a clear warning as to recognition evidence and the risk of mistake.

11.—ABUSE OF PROCESS

In *Warren and others v Attorney General for Jersey* [2011] UKPC 10; [2011] 3   **39–32**
W.L.R. 464, prosecution evidence had been obtained by officers of the Jersey police who had used an audio device without obtaining the consent of two foreign authorities and who had misled the French authorities with respect to a tracking device. The Privy Council, concluding that *R. v Grant* [2006] Q.B. 60 was wrongly decided, dismissed the appeals against a decision to refuse to stay the prosecutions on the ground of abuse of process. The Privy Council concluded that the Court exercised a broad discretion when determining whether to stay criminal proceedings as an abuse of process on the ground of executive misconduct. It would have regard to the individual circumstances of the particular case and strike a balance between the public interest of ensuring that those accused of grave crimes were prosecuted and the competing public interest of ensuring that the misconduct did not undermine public confidence in the criminal justice system and bring it into disrepute.

Warren is discussed in the International Journal of Evidence & Proof, Volume 13, Number 4, at pp.268–271.

In *R. v Daniels* [2010] EWCA Crim 2740; [2011] Crim. L.R. 556, a number of men, including the appellant, faced charges of murder, conspiracy to rob, or both. One of the accused, S, entered into an agreement shortly before trial pursuant to s.73 of the Serious Organised Crime and Police Act 2005 under which he agreed to give assistance to the authorities. S gave evidence for the Crown. The central issue before the Court of Appeal was whether it was an abuse of process for the case to proceed on S's evidence and/or whether his evidence should have been excluded under s.78 of the Police and Criminal Evidence Act 1984. The Court held that S's evidence was not wrongly admitted at the trial. The commentary on the judgment in the Crim. L.R. begins "What price justice?" This is an early indication of the criticism to follow.

13.—CIVIL PROCEEDINGS

(b) *The civil justice reforms*

O'Brien v Chief Constable of South Wales Police (see n.204) also reported at [2005]   **39–35**
2 A.C. 534.

CHAPTER 40

AUTHORSHIP AND EXECUTION, ATTESTATION, ANCIENT DOCUMENTS, CONNECTED AND INCORPORATED DOCUMENTS, ALTERATIONS AND BLANKS, REGISTRATION, STAMPS, ETC.

(c) *Presumption in favour of authenticity*

It is not incumbent on the disclosing party to seek an admission of authenticity.   **40–04**

1.—GENUINENESS, AUTHORSHIP AND EXECUTION

(iii) *Mode of signature*

fn.19 *Re Parsons* [2002] WTLR 237.   **40–08**

(v) *Qualified signature: procuration: agency*

fn.52 (Correction). See below, para.40–15   **40–11**

(c) *Deeds, signature, sealing and delivery*

(i) *The law prior to the Law of Property (Miscellaneous Provisions) Act 1989*

fn.87 (Correction). See below, para.40–33.   **40–17**

(ii) *The law subsequent to the Law of Property (Miscellaneous Provisions) Act 1989*

See *Mercury Tax Group Ltd & Anor, R (on the application of) v HM Commissioners*   **40–20**
of Revenue & Customs & Ors [2008] EWHC 2721: the signature and attestation must
form part of the same physical document which constitutes the deed.)

(iii) *Company contracts and the execution of documents by companies*

40–23   Pursuant to s44(5) of the Companies Act 2006, in favour of a purchaser in good faith for valuable consideration the document is deemed to have been duly executed by a company, if it purports to be signed in accordance with s44(2). See *Lovett v. Carson County Homes Ltd* [2009] EWHC 1143(Ch); [2009] BCLC 196 at [79] for the proposition that "purports" in s44(5) "operates to refer to the impression a document conveys" focusing on what appears to be the case rather than what actually is the case.

fn.127 See *Williams & Ors v Redcard Ltd & Ors* [2011] EWCA Civ 466: in order to comply with s44(4), the signatures on behalf of the verndor company did not need to spell out that those signatures were "by or on behalf of" the company, it was sufficient to use the phrase "Seller" above the signatures. However the Court did state, obiter, that:

> ". . . long drawn-out litigation about the execution of a document by a company can be avoided by taking more care over compliance with the formalities at the time of execution by, for example, adding words that expressly state the capacity in which an individual is signing a document to which a company is a party."
> (Para.30); *ANZ Banking Group Ltd v Australian Glass & Mirrors Pty Ltd* (1991) 4 A.C.S.R. 14 SC (Vic).

3.—ALTERATIONS: ERASURES

(a) *Deeds and contracts*

40–45   fn.295 See also *Mercury Tax Group Ltd & Anor, R (on the application of) v HM Commissioners of Revenue & Customs & Ors* [2008] EWHC 2721 which considered *Koenigsblatt v. Sweet* [1923] 2 Ch 314 and *Raiffeisen Zentralbank Osterreich AG v Crossseas Shipping Ltd* [2000] 1 W.L.R. 1135 CA.

CHAPTER 41

DOCUMENTS AND DOCUMENTARY EVIDENCE; HOW DOCUMENTARY EVIDENCE IS PROVED; CATEGORIES OF DOCUMENTARY EVIDENCE: PUBLIC, JUDICIAL, PRIVATE

1.—DOCUMENTS AND DOCUMENTARY EVIDENCE EXPLAINED

(a) *Document defined*

In the Identity Cards Act 2006, s.41(1) the term "document" "includes a stamp or label".   **41–01**

Footnote 21: Cp. *Taylor v DPP* LTL 20/10/2009

(b) *Document: real of documentary evidence?*

In *PPS v Duddy* [2009] N.I. 19 at [29] a breath test certificate was held to be real   **41–02**
evidence because it represented the automatic calculations of a machine from the defendant's breath.

(c) *The original document rule*

For a discussion of the format in which computer documents should be produced   **41–03**
to an opponent and as evidence at trial see R. Champion, "Electronic documents in construction litigation: lessons from experience" [2011] Construction Law Journal 227, 231 et seq.

Footnote 40: In Scotland the best evidence rule is still relevant, see *Liquidator of Letham Grange Dev. Co. Ltd. v. Foxworth Investments Ltd* [2011]CSOH 66 at [94].

(d) *Demise of the original document rule*

(i) *At common law*

fn.62 This passage was endorsed in *PPS v Duddy* [2009] N.I. 19 at [28].   **41–04**

(ii) *Statutory abolition*

41–05   In *Ventouris v Mountain (No.2)* [1992] 1 WLR 887 at 901, Staughton L.J. said that the word "production" in s.8(1)(b) of the Civil Evidence Act 1995 does:

> "not refer to counsel handing the document to the court, but to a witness who is qualified to do so in accordance with the rules of evidence producing the document and saying what it is. Authentication is concerned only with the issue whether the copy is a true copy of the absent original, and not with what the original was."

41–06   In *PPS v Duddy* [2009] N.I. 19, a drink-driving case from Northern Ireland, the original certificate setting out a machine's analysis of the defendant's breath had been lost . The police officer who had administered the breath test produced a photocopy and testified that it was genuine. The magistrate held the copy inadmissible under Criminal Justice (Evidence)(Northern Ireland) Order 2004 art. 36, which is worded identically to s.133 of the Criminal Justice Act 2003, as he had not made the copy and the person who made the copy had not been produced as a witness. Quite apart from this, as a matter of discretion, the magistrate said he would have refused to admit the copy because it was of poor quality, notice to adduce the copy had not been served on the defendant and the original could still not be found. The Court of Appeal in Northern Ireland said that the results of the breath test could have been proved by oral evidence alone and that if the prosecution chose to tender documentary evidence, a copy was no less admissible than the original document. The police officer's testimony had adequately authenticated the copy. According to Kerr LCJ (*ibid* at [27]), there was no:

> "warrant for concluding that because evidence was not available from the person who actually copied the original that it should be deemed inadmissible on that account . . . [T]here is no sensible reason that evidence from the police officer that the document was an exact copy of that which he had completed should not be sufficient to authenticate it."

Just as a film or photograph can be proved by any person who was present when it was taken or who recognizes its contents without having to call the film-maker (*R v Murphy* [1990] NI 306), the officer could authenticate the copy by testifying that it was recognized by him as an exact copy.

It was an improper exercise of discretion to have refused to admit the evidence from the reasons given by the magistrate. Neither failure to give notice of an intention to produce a copy nor the poor quality of a legible copy is a ground for exclusion (*ibid* at [31]). Furthermore, the discretion conferred by PACE to exclude prosecution evidence was conferred on the court to avoid injustice or unfairness in the trial process, not to penalize the prosecuting authorities or the police service for their handling of evidence (*ibid* at [32]).

(e) *Authentication of documents*

(i) *Generally*

41–07   Where a party relies on a document written in a foreign language, to save time and expense, its translation should be agreed, if possible and, if not, settled at a case management hearing before the trial: *Gemstar-TV Guide International Inc v Virgin Media Ltd* [2011] EWCA Civ. 302 at [11].

(vii) *Interlocutory proceedings*   **41–28b**

In *Liquidator of Letham Grange Dev. Co. Ltd. v. Foxworth Investments Ltd* [2011] CSOH 66 at [94] Lord Glennie said:

> ". . . if a party leads oral evidence as to the content of the document, or leads evidence by reference to a copy of a document, and the other party does not object, then the party leading it cannot subsequently complain about its admission on the basis of the best evidence rule."

CHAPTER 42

EXCLUSION OF EXTRINSIC EVIDENCE IN SUBSTITUTION OF, TO CONTRADICT, VARY, OR ADD TO DOCUMENTS

4.—EXCEPTIONS TO THE RULE

(e) *Rent Acts, etc.*

(v) *Principal or agent*

fn.244 See also *Internaut Shipping Ltd GmbH and another v Fercometal SARL* [2003] EWCA Civ 812.   **42–36**

(f) *Invalid or conditional documents: escrows: fraud: mistake: want of consideration, etc.*

(v) *Recitals, preambles, etc.*

n.213: See also *OTV Birwelco Ltd v Technical and General Guarantee Co* [2002] EWHC 2240.   **42–46**

CHAPTER 43

JUDGMENTS

2.—JUDGMENTS AS GIVING RISE TO ESTOPPELS IN SUBSEQUENT PROCEEDINGS

Judgments include consent orders (*Kinch v Walcott* [1929] AC 482) and settlements **43–03** contained in Tomlin orders (*Zurich Insurance Company Plc v Hayward* [2011] EWCA Civ 641).

(a) *All judgments are impeachable on certain grounds*

(i) *Not final*

fn.20 A judgment is not final until an order is drawn which embodies the decision **43–05** as a matter of record, as prior to this, the Court could recall its judgment, or parts of it, before the order is drawn, although the circumstances in which that can be done are limited. (See B*T Pension Scheme Trustees Ltd v British Telecommunications Plc & Anor* [2011] EWHC 2071, para.57.)

fn.36 There is well-established authority that where a final decision has been made by a court a challenge to the decision on the basis that it has been obtained by fraud must be made by a fresh action alleging and proving the fraud: *Flower v Lloyd* (1877) 6 Ch.D. 297; *Jonesco v Beard* [1930] AC 298; *Kuwait Airways Corporation v Iraqi Airways (No 8)* [2001] 1 WLR 429; *Owens v Noble* [2010] EWCA Civ 224.

(iv) *Obtained by fraud or collusion*

Foreign judgments as a matter of common law may also be impeached if recogni- **43–08** tion would be contrary to public policy (Dicey & Morris: The Conflict of Laws, 14th edn. Rule 44).

fn.76

> "Issue estoppel operates regardless of whether or not an English court would regard the reasoning of the foreign judgment as open to criticism."
> per Lord Diplock in *The Sennar (No. 2)* [1985] 1 WLR 490 (HL) at 493. See also *Yukos Capital SARL v OJSC Rosneft Oil Company* [2011] EWHC 1461 (Comm), paras.66–69.

(d) *Judgments in civil cases as affecting parties and privies*

(iii) *Res judicata estoppels*

43–24   **Scope of the rule.** The principle that estoppels arise from a judgment in previous litigation between the same parties also applies in the civil context to non-statutory disciplinary proceedings: *Coke- Wallis, R (on the application of) v Institute of Chartered Accountants in England and Wales* [2011] UKSC 1, [2011] 2 All ER 1.

43–26   See *Molnlycke Health Care Ab & Anor v BSN Medical Ltd & Anor* [2009] EWHC 3370 (Pat) where two entities, which were subsidiaries of the same holding company, but where party A had granted an exclusive licence to party B, were held not to be the same party for the purpose of article 27.

43–41   fn.317 See *Yukos Capital SARL v OJSC Rosneft Oil Company* [2011] EWHC 1461 (Comm).

43–43   In *Coke-Wallis, R (on the application of) v Institute of Chartered Accountants in England and Wales* [2011] UKSC 1, [2011] 2 All ER 1, the Institute raised the novel point that:

"... given the disciplinary context the Supreme Court should recognise a public interest exception to the strict application of the doctrine of cause of action estoppel which is absent in the case of conventional civil litigation. This was prompted by a suggestion made by Lord Phillips in the course of the argument that an absolute principle of the kind adverted to by Lord Keith in Arnold would or might put the safety of the public at risk. So, for example, if such an absolute rule applied to doctors it might put the lives of patients at risk ..."

The Supreme Court concluded that:

"... I see the force of the introduction of such a principle. However, whether and in what circumstances to permit such an exception seems to me to be essentially a matter for Parliament and not for the courts ..." (paras 48–50).

43–45   See *BT Pension Scheme Trustees Ltd v British Telecommunications Plc & Anor* [2011] EWHC 2071 where the Court stated:

"... The [abuse of process] doctrine is generally applied in a second case in relation to what ought to have gone in prior litigation, but I do not see why the principle should not be held to apply, if appropriate, to a case where an action is heard in more than one phase, though it will generally be unnecessary to do so because other considerations (such as the state of the pleadings) will usually deal with any problems ..." (para.61).

43–46   fn.340 See *El Diwany v Hansen & Anor* [2011] EWHC 2077 (QB):

"... Mere re-litigation in circumstances not giving rise to cause of action estoppel or issue estoppel does not necessarily give rise to abuse of the process. Some additional element is required such as collateral attack on a previous decision, or unjust harassment or oppression of the other party." (para.65.)

(e) *Criminal Cases*

(v) *Oppression*

fn.460 In *Yam v R.* [2010] EWCA Crim 2072, the Court of Appeal, approved the   **43–73**
decision in Humphyrs, and went on to state that

> ". . . the power to prevent an abuse of the process of the court where a further trial
> would be unfair or oppressive we assume for the purposes of this case does survive
> and is consistent with the majority view in Humphrys . . ." (para.10).

3.—JUDGMENTS AS EVIDENCE AGAINST STRANGERS

(b) *At common law*

(i) *Principle*

See *PM, R (on the application of) v Hertfordshire County Council* [2010] EWHC   **43–79**
2056 where, citing passages from Ch.43 of *Phipson*, the Court held that the local
council was not entitled to simply adopt the decision of the First-tier Tribunal as to
the age of the Claimant, as the Council was a stranger to those proceedings.

(c) *Acquittals*

(i) *Other exceptions*

fn.524 the correct citation is [2000] All ER (D) 1568.   **43–85**

(e) *Under the Police and Criminal Evidence Act 1984 sections 73 to 75*

fn.594 In *R v Downer* [2009] EWCA Crim 1361 the Court concluded that evidence   **43–94**
of the earlier guilty pleas should have been excluded under s78.
fn.595 See *C v R.* [2010] EWCA Crim 2971 where the Lord Chief Justice stated:

> ". . . he evidential presumption is that the conviction truthfully reflects the fact that
> the defendant committed the offence. Equally, however, it is clear that the defendant
> cannot be prevented from seeking to demonstrate that he did not in fact commit the
> offence and therefore, that the jury in the current trial should disregard the conviction
> . . ." (para.9).

CHAPTER 44

APPENDIX
MISCELLANEOUS STATUTES, RULES ETC.[1]

Note: Up-to-date versions of the Civil Procedure Rules can be found at http:// justice.gov.uk/guidance/courts-and-tribunals/courts/procedure-rules/civil/index.htm [Accessed August 25, 2011]; up-to-date versions of the Criminal Procedure Rules can be found at http://justice.gov.uk/guidance/courts-and-tribunals/courts/procedure-rules/criminal/index.htm [Accessed August 25, 2011].

Civil Evidence Act 1968

PART II.—MISCELLANEOUS AND GENERAL

Convictions, etc. as evidence in civil proceedings

11. Convictions as evidence in civil proceedings

Note the amendments to s.11, whereby references to "court-martial" are replaced by references to "service offence," together with the consequential insertion of a new subsection (7).[2]   **44–06**

16. Abolition of certain privileges

Subsection (4) and the words after "adultery" in subsection (5) are spent.   **44–10**

---

[1] Statutory provisions, Civil and Criminal Procedure Rules, etc. are now very widely available online. They are also periodically amended. For these reasons, only a range of older statutory provisions is now included in this Appendix. These remain as set out in the seventeenth edition as we go to press, but owing to periodic amendments readers are advised always to check on the latest text.
[2] This new subsection being reflected in the amended s.13(4). See also s.18(2) and the newly inserted s.18(2A) on the meaning of "service court".